Josef Moser

Ubuntu 22.04

Quick Guide
for Beginners

[JMP]

Illustration: Josef Moser
Cover Design: Jutta Moser and Josef Moser

Publisher:
[JMP] Josef Moser Publishing, Ulmenstr. 55, 90537 Feucht

Production: Amazon
KDPISBN: 9798359207959

Table of contents

1. Foreword 11
2. What is Linux? 13
3. What is Ubuntu? 15
4. How do I get Ubuntu? 18
5. Creating a bootable Stick 20
6. Starting from the Stick 21
7. Installation 22

    7.1. Keyboard Layout 24
    7.2. Installation Selection 25

        7.2.1. Type of Installation 25
        7.2.2. Other options 26

    7.3. Create Partitions 27

        7.3.1. Automatic Partitioning 27
        7.3.2. Individual Partitioning 30

            7.3.2.1. EFI partition 32
            7.3.2.2. Root Partition (root directory) 33
            7.3.2.3. Home Directory 34
            7.3.2.4. Swap 36

        7.3.3. Advanced Features 37

    7.4. Set up the Time Zone 38
    7.5. Personalisation 39
    7.6. The Installation 40
    7.7. First Start 41

8. First Steps in Ubuntu 22.04 42

    8.1. Connect to Online Accounts 42
    8.2. Ubuntu Data Collection 43
    8.3. Privacy 44
    8.4. Ready to go 45

9. Software Updater 46

10. The GNOME Desktop.. 47

    10.1. The Dock.. 47

        10.1.1. Preset 47

        10.1.2. Configuration of the Dock....................... 49

        10.1.3. Removing Application Launchers.............. 49

        10.1.4. Adding application launchers 50

        10.1.5. Order of Application Launchers.............. 50

    10.2. Applications Overview 51

    10.3. The Top Panel.. 54

        10.3.1. Activities Overview.................................. 55

        10.3.2. Workspaces.. 56

        10.3.3. Clock and Notifications 58

        10.3.4. Status Menu 59

    10.4. Preinstalled Applications 60

        10.4.1. Office Applications.................................. 60

            10.4.1.1. LibreOffice.................................. 60

            10.4.1.2. Document Viewer 65

        10.4.2. Multimedia.. 66

        10.4.3. Graphics Applications 67

        10.4.4. Internet.. 69

            10.4.4.1. Thunderbird 69

            10.4.4.2. Firefox 70

        10.4.5. Utilities 71

            10.4.5.1. Passwords and Keys 71

            10.4.5.2. Backups 74

            10.4.5.3. Text Editor Gedit 77

            10.4.5.4. Disks... 78

            10.4.5.5. System Monitor 79

        10.4.6. Games 80

11. Software and Updates 81

    11.1. Ubuntu Applications.. 81
    11.2. Updates... 82
    11.3. Additional Drivers 83
    11.4. Livepatch 84

12. Software Center (Ubuntu Software).. 85

    12.1. Installing Applications.. 85
    12.2. Remove Applications 89

13. Snap Store 90
14. Flatpaks 92
15. PPA (Personal Package Archive) 94
16. Alternative Installation Options... 95

    16.1. Synaptic Package Manager.. 96
    16.2. Terminal 99

17. The File Manager (Nautilus) 100

    17.1. Overview.. 100
    17.2. Configuration of the Home Folder............................... 105

        17.2.1. Overview 105
        17.2.2. Create a new Folder 108
        17.2.3. Hiding the directory list...................................... 109
        17.2.4. Enlarge the Icons.. 109
        17.2.5. Create Bookmarks... 109
        17.2.6. Show hidden Files 110
        17.2.7. File Manager Settings... 111

18. Settings... 113

    18.1. Network.. 114
    18.2. Bluetooth... 114
    18.3. Background 114
    18.4. Appearance... 115

        18.4.1. Style and Accent Colors 115
        18.4.2. Dock 116

18.5. Notifications 117

18.6. Search 118

18.7. Applications 119

18.8. Privacy 120

18.9. Online Accounts 121

18.10. Sharing.. 121

18.11. Sound.. 122

18.12. Power.. 124

18.13. Display 125

18.14. Mouse and Touchpad.................................... 127

18.15. Keyboard 127

18.16. Printer 128

18.17. Removable Media 128

18.18. Region and Language 129

18.19. Accessibility.. 130

18.20. Users 131

18.21. About.. 132

18.22. Default Applications...................................... 133

18.23. Date and Time 134

19. GNOME Tweaks... 135

19.1. Appearance.. 136

19.2. Windows... 137

19.3. Windows Titlebars 137

19.3.1. Titlebar Buttons................................... 138

19.4. Top Bar... 138

19.5. Fonts 139

19.6. Startup Applications....................................... 140

19.7. Keyboard and Mouse 141

20. Extensions... 142

20.1.1. Extensions via browser add-on 143

20.1.2. Extensions in Synaptic.......................... 144

20.1.3. The Arc Menu 145

21. Synchronisation with the smartphone 146

22. Useful additional Programs 147

   22.1. Office 147

      22.1.1. Focuswriter.. 147

      22.1.2. Scribus 148

      22.1.3. Calibre 149

      22.1.4. Text Editor Nano..................................... 150

   22.2. Graphics... 151

      22.2.1. GIMP... 151

      22.2.2. Darktable... 152

      22.2.3. Krita 153

      22.2.4. Other Graphics Programs.......................... 154

   22.3. Video Editing.. 155

      22.3.1. KDENLIVE... 155

      22.3.2. OpenShot 156

      22.3.3. Other video editing programmes 156

   22.4. Audio 157

      22.4.1. Audacity 157

      22.4.2. Ardour... 158

      22.4.3. MuseScore 159

   22.5. Internet 160

   22.6. Audio and Video Player 161

   22.7. Third-party Software 162

23. Windows Programs in Linux 163

   23.1. Wine and PlayOnLinux 163

   23.2. Virtual Machine (Virtual Box) 166

24. The Terminal.. 169

25. Ubuntu Flavours 171

26. Outlook.. 172

1. Foreword

Many computer users are mainly familiar with Microsoft Windows or Apple MacOS.

Linux is generally considered to be difficult to access and only suitable for hobbyists and tinkerers.

I would like to show in my quick guide that you do not have to be afraid to deal with this operating system.

Linux distributions have now reached a very high level. This applies not only to the operating system itself, but also to the available applications.

Libre Office, for example, is a very good alternative to Microsoft Office.

There also are many very good applications for photo and film editing.

It is possible to edit photos and organize them in many different ways.

You can still use Firefox and Thunderbird to browse the web and check your emails.

Currently there are over 100 Linux distributions available to choose from.

This may be confusing to potential newcomers.

This book is intended to give you a quick and easy access to **Ubuntu 22.04**.

After some basic information this book will guide you through the operating system step by step.

I concentrate on the essential elements that are important for a home user.

After reading this book, you will be able to

- get an installation medium (ISO file) for Ubuntu 22.04
- install Ubuntu 22.04
- understand the basic settings of Ubuntu 22.04
- configure Ubuntu 22.04 to suit your needs

I would be very pleased, if I manage to get you excited about Linux in this way.

You may be surprised at the benefits a Linux system can bring.

With this in mind I hope you enjoy this book and the Linux operating system **Ubuntu 22.04**.

Josef Moser

2. What is Linux?

Linux is a family of free and open-source software opera-ting systems based on the Linux Kernel, an operating system kernel first released on September 17, 1991 by Linus Torvalds. Linux is typically packaged in a Linux distribution (or distro for short).
Distributions include the Linux kernel and supporting system software and libraries, many of which are provided by the GNU Project.
(Source: Wikipedia.org)

The Linux kernel saw the light of day in 1991 in version 0.0.1. Linus Torvalds, who is still in charge of kernel development today, had no idea what he would initiate with the release of his small hobby project.

Today, the term Linux is usually used as a synonym for the entire system. Strictly speaking, however, only the kernel is called Linux.
Only when combined with applications and programs that follow the GNU guidelines it becomes the system we know and love today.

The first Linux distributions were released in 1994.
They had made it their business to develop usable systems as an alternative to Windows and MacOS:

- Debian
- Suse
- Slackware
- RedHat

A major step forward was the release of **Open Office** (Version 1) in 2002.

It was a full-featured open source office suite, which was available free of charge.

Of course, the functionality was still limited compared to Microsoft Office, but Open Office became better and better over time.

Libre Office has been developed at a later time as an independent fork of Open Office. This extensive and meanwhile very mature office suite is pre-installed in **Ubuntu 22.04**.

Meanwhile there are countless variants of Linux distributions. However, most of them are based on Debian, OpenSUSE, Ubuntu, Arch Linux, Gentoo or Red Hat.

3. What is Ubuntu?

The Linux operating system **Ubuntu** has been around since 2004.
The Ubuntu project was founded by Marc Shuttleworth, a South African multimillionaire who is also the main sponsor through his company **Canonical.**

The name means something like "humanity" or "public spirit" in the Zulu language.
Thus, the project focuses on developing an operating system that should be available to as many people as possible all over the world.

Particular attention was paid to intuitive usability and accessibility.
Ubuntu is free and open source software that is available free of charge.

The level of awareness and popularity has increased steadily since the first version was released.

Ubuntu is based on **Debian**. This means that the package management created by Debian and also the software selection have been adopted.
However, both distributions evolved away from each other over time.
Ubuntu was often accused of being too commercially oriented, while Debian continued to follow the philosophy of open source and therefore refused to accept some innovations that Ubuntu introduced.

In April and October of each year, a new Ubuntu version is released, which receives **support for 9 months.**

It is named after the *year* and *month of* publication.

Ubuntu 21.10 was released in October (**10**) of 2021 (**21**) and is now no longer supported.

> **Support** *means that the operating system receives updates from Ubuntu in the form of security updates and bug fixes.*

However, every two years (even years!) a special version is released that will receive **support from** Ubuntu for a period of **5 years.**

This is called an **LTS version**.

LTS stands for **Long-Term Support**.

The current LTS-version is **Ubuntu 22.04**.

Support for this version will end after 5 years in **April 2027**.

The next LTS version **Ubuntu 24.04** will be released in **April 2024.**

Support for this version will end after 5 years in **April 2029.**

All other versions are supported for 9 months.

- **Ubuntu 18.04 LTS**   supported until 04/2023
- Ubuntu 21.10   supported until 07/2022
- **Ubuntu 20.04 LTS**   supported until 04/2025
- Ubuntu 22.10   supported until 07/2023
- Ubuntu 23.04   supported until 01/2024

The advantage of the short-term supported systems is that the software they contain is usually more up-to-date than that of the last regular LTS edition.

With LTS versions, the operating system remains essentially in the state in which it was delivered for five years.
Updates only include bug fixes and security patches.
This may be too conservative for some users in the long run.
However, the older a software is, the more it is tested and therefore more stable.

Newer versions of applications, such as those included in the short-term supported versions, may be more unstable because the testing period was shorter.

In this guide I describe **Ubuntu 22.04 LTS**.
However, much of this is also applicable to **Ubuntu 22.10** and possibly **Ubuntu 23.04.**

It is recommended for beginners to try the LTS version first.
An intermediate version makes sense if the LTS version does not optimally support your hardware.

In addition the official names, which refer to the release date, Ubuntu versions always have an additional fantasy name.
Ubuntu 22.04 is called **Jammy Jellyfish**.

4. How do I get Ubuntu?

It is always the safest way to obtain the required installation medium (ISO file) directly from Ubuntu.
This can be found on the **Ubuntu homepage** under **Downloads**.

  https://www.ubuntu.com/download/desktop

The easy way: Push the green **Download Button**.
Right beneath you can see „See our alternative Downloads".
Here you will find the Network Installer, older Versions of Ubuntu and BitTorrents.
You also can select another **mirror** to increase the Download speed.

System requirements:

2 GHz Dual Core Processor or better
4 GB RAM or better
25 GB free hard disk space or more
DVD drive or USB connection
Internet connection

However, these are minimum requirements.
For smooth working, better equipment is recommended.

Other Ubuntu distributions

There are also other variants (flavours) of Ubuntu available for download.
These are stand-alone Ubuntu distributions with alternative desktops.
For example, there are:

- Kubuntu with KDE Plasma Desktop
- Xubuntu with XFCE desktop
- Ubuntu Mate with Mate Desktop
- Ubuntu Budgie with Budgie Desktop
- Lubuntu with LXQt desktop
- Ubuntu Studio

The basic system is almost identical in all these versions, but the user interface is designed very differently in each case.

The LTS versions of these so-called "flavours" are only supported for 3 years, in contrast to the main version.
The intermediate versions adhere to the 9-month cycle.

You can try out these variants if you don't like the design of the main version for some reason.

An overview of the different Ubuntu flavours can be found at the end of the book.

5. Creating a bootable Stick

After you have downloaded the **ISO file**, you need to create a **bootable stick.**
This means that you prepare a USB stick so that you can start Ubuntu with it.
For this task you need an appropriate application.
There are several applications you can use for this task.
Etcher is a good choice in my opinion.
Etcher is available free of charge for Linux, Windows and MacOS.
https://www.balena.io/etcher/
Download Etcher and then create the stick.

Select Image: Select the ISO file for Ubuntu 22.04
Select Drive: You will see a selection of sticks that you have plugged into a free USB port
Flash: Start!

Double-check whether the right stick is selected!
Any content on the stick will be completely deleted during this process!

6. Starting from the Stick

You plug the stick into a free USB port and after restarting the computer, it will automatically recognise that a bootable stick is present.

In this case, the live system of Ubuntu starts immediately.
For this, however, it is necessary that the stick is in first place in the boot sequence in the **BIOS.**
If, for example, the hard disk is in first place, the operating system on it is always started and the stick is ignored.

If this is the case, you must change the **boot sequence in** the **BIOS.**

You can usually access the BIOS via one of the F keys (for example [F2]). While the computer is booting, you must press this key several times. This will prevent the computer to boot and takes you to the BIOS instead.

Please refer to the manual to find out which button is the right one for your mainboard. It varies depending on the manufacturer.
There is a menu somewhere in the BIOS called **Boot** (or similar).
Here you can usually see the boot order and change it if necessary.

7. Installation

After successfully launching the ISO file from your stick, you select your language.

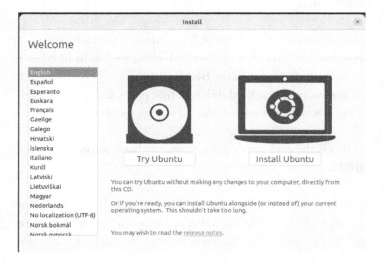

On the left-hand side, first set the desired language.
As English is usually the default language at this point, activate another language by scrolling in the menu until it is selectable.
You can now choose whether you want to try Ubuntu first or install it straight away.
I would recommend to start the **Live System** by selecting **Try Ubuntu**.
The advantage of this is that you can get an overview of the system without having to install Ubuntu on the hard disk.
The **Live System** is and remains on the stick and therefore does not change anything on your PC.

Nevertheless, you can explore the system, configure it and even install applications.

However, changes in the live system are not permanently saved, so any actions you perform will become invalid after a restart.

If you have decided to install **Ubuntu 22.04** on your computer, select either **Install Ubuntu 22.04 LTS** or, after a restart, the **Install Ubuntu** button in the window shown above instead of **Try Ubuntu**.

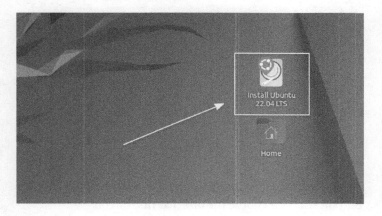

In the picture above you can see the button on the desktop of the Live System that you can use to start the Installation of **Ubuntu 22.04 LTS.**

7.1. Keyboard Layout

In the next window, select the **Keyboard Layout.**

As the keyboard layouts are different in every country, it is important that you choose the one that fits for you.

The keyboard layout is preset in the language you have selected before.

Nevertheless, the selection can still be refined at this point.

It is recommended that you use a sample text to check whether the chosen model meets all your requirements.

Type text to test the keyboard.

This way you can immediately see whether the individual letters including special characters are displayed correctly.

Take your time at this point.

7.2. Installation Selection

7.2.1. Type of Installation

The following window offers you some basic alternatives and choices regarding the type of installation.

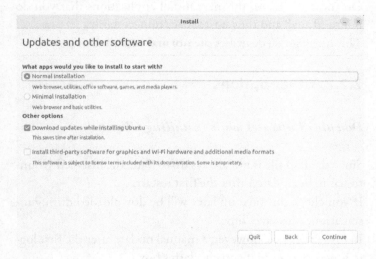

You can choose between

- Normal installation
- Minimal installation

Minimal installation
No applications are pre-installed.
This gives you a leaner basic system, which you can expand at a later time according to your individual needs.

Normal installation

Certain standard applications, such as the Libre-Office package, are already pre-installed, so you can start working right away.

The normal installation is convenient because it takes the basic decisions off your hands.

On the other hand, this may install applications that you do not need at all and thus waste space unnecessarily.

This quick guide describes the **normal installation.**

7.2.2. Other options

Download updates while installing Ubuntu

Since the ISO file is not always up to date, the installed Ubuntu has to be updated after the first restart.

If you check this box, updates will be downloaded during installation. This saves time.

In my experience, however, a manual update after the first login is necessary even if you check this box.

Install third-party software for graphics and WiFi hardware and additional media formats

Here you will be asked if you want to install third-party software or not.

Since this type of software may not be pre-installed Linux distributions for licensing reasons, it is up to you whether you need and want to use proprietary drivers and codecs.

In particular, graphics cards and WLAN cards run better and more smoothly with the third-party software provided.

7.3. Create Partitions

7.3.1. Automatic Partitioning

So far nothing has been changed on your hard disk.
However, this changes with the next steps.
Partitioning prepares the selected hard disk for the installation of Ubuntu.

Partitioning: the space available on the hard disk is divided into different areas (partitions) and these are adapted in a further step for the installation.

I always recommend that beginners provide a separate hard drive for a Linux system.
Although with some experience dual-boot and even multi-boot on a single hard drive is not a problem, there may be some difficulties that may present a novice user with major hurdles.

If there is a hard disk with Windows in your computer, disconnect it temporarily for security reasons so that you don't accidentally delete your Windows system.

The following options are shown as installation types:

- Erase disk and install Ubuntu
- Something else

Erase disk and install Ubuntu

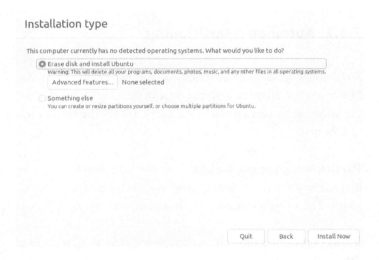

Start the installation with **Install now**.
This starts the automatic partitioning.
In the next window you will be informed that the changes will
be written to your hard disk in the next step.
All data on it will be deleted.

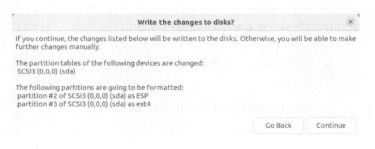

So please make sure once again that you have selected the correct hard disk and that no data loss will occur if you now press **Next.**

Install Ubuntu next to Windows

If you have decided to install Ubuntu on a single hard disk alongside an existing Windows, the installation programme will automatically detect that there is already an operating system (namely Windows) on the hard disk.

*In this case, you will be asked whether you want to delete the hard disk or install **Ubuntu alongside Windows.***

However, Windows is not automatically recognised when booting.

To do this, the file /etc/default/grub must be edited.

Add GRUB_DISABLE_OS_PROBER=false to this file.

After **sudo update-grub,** Windows should be recognised.

If you have selected automatic partitioning, you can jump to **chapter 7.4** at this point to continue the installation.

*If you select **Something else**, you can create the partitions manually and thus adapt them even further to your individual needs. This procedure is described in chapter 7.3.2.*

7.3.2. Individual Partitioning

Individual partitioning makes sense especially if, for example, you want to decouple your **home directory** (personal folder) from the operating system or define the sizes of the individual partitions yourself.
As already mentioned, select **Something else** for this procedure when asked about the installation type.

The first window that opens in this case shows you which hard disks are currently installed in your computer and are therefore available for selection.

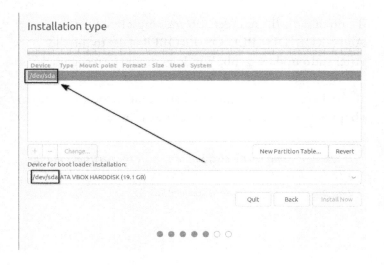

The abbreviation **dev** stands for device.
The abbreviation **sd** stands for hard disk.
sda is therefore hard disk **a**.

Another hard disk would be called **sdb.**

If there are several hard disks in the computer, you must select at this time which one should be partitioned.

Be very careful because partitioning permanently deletes all files.

After you have made the correct selection, create a **partition table**.

To do this, press the corresponding button at the bottom right.

New partition table

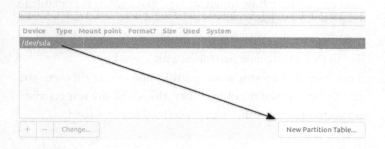

If there are already partitions on this hard disk, they will be overwritten during this process.

This will be indicated again in the next window.

Confirm with **Next.**

Installation type

You can see here how much storage space (MB) is available in total on the hard disk.
You can now use this proportionately as you like.
To do this, create new partitions with the + **key.**
The difference to automatic partitioning is that this way you can determine the number of partitions and the respective sizes yourself, while otherwise predefined sizes are used.

7.3.2.1. EFI partition

*For UEFI installations you **also** need an EFI partition!*

***250 MB** should be sufficient for this partition.*

Create the **EFI system partition** first before continuing with the other partitions!
You will find the selection in **Use as**.

You can skip this point if you are doing a BIOS installation!

7.3.2.2. Root Partition (root directory)

Use the **[+]** button to create a partition.

Size:	⬚ | − + MB
Type for the new partition:	⦿ Primary
	◯ Logical
Location for the new partition:	⦿ Beginning of this space
	◯ End of this space
Use as:	Ext4 journaling file system ⌄
Mount point:	/ ⌄
	Cancel OK

You create a partition that will contain the operating system.
This partition is called the **root partition**.
To be prepared for the future, you should choose a size of at least 20 GB for the operating system itself. This corresponds to 20000 MB.
Select **Primary** as the **type of the new partition**.
You need logical partitions if you want to create more than four partitions.

For **using as** select
Ext4 journaling file system.

As **mount point,** select
/ .
Now you will be redirected back to the first window.

The partition for the root directory is now visible as a green bar in the graphic.
The size you have assigned for this partition will also be displayed.

You can now proceed in the same way with the remaining available memory.

7.3.2.3. Home Directory

You press the [+] button again and repeat the previous steps.

Now create the **Home Directory**.
Your personal data will be stored here.
This includes all the documents you create, but also configuration files.

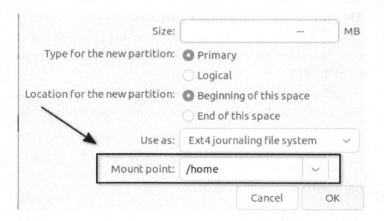

For **using as** select
Ext4 journaling file system.

Depending on what you intend to do with your computer, the size of this partition should be generous.
Use the remaining available memory space for this.
As **mount point** select
/home.

Click OK to confirm.
After confirming with OK, you should see the following window.

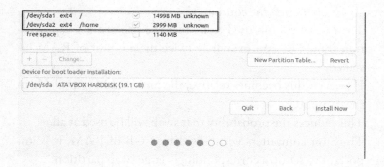

The created partitions are marked by different colours.
Further information about the size of the partitions and the mount points can be found below.
If you discover a mistake at this point, you can correct it at any time by clicking the **Back** button.
If not, confirm with
Install now.

You now can continue with the installation process.

7.3.2.4. Swap

Ubuntu creates a swap file.
You should only create your own swap partition if you want to determine the size of the swap space yourself.
If the built-in memory in the computer is not sufficient for certain actions, the swap area on the hard disk is used as extended memory.
If you notice that this happens more often, you should think about upgrading the computer.
The rule of thumb used to be that the size of the swap partition should be approximately twice the amount of RAM installed.
However, this becomes relative, the more RAM is available in the computer.
This reduces the probability that swap will be used at all.
Thus, on computers with less than 4 GB of RAM, it is important to set up a correspondingly large swap partition.
Swap becomes less important if you have 16 GB or more in your computer.

If you have selected automatic installation, Ubuntu creates an appropriately sized swap file.
If you only define the root and home partitions during manual installation, a swap file is also created automatically.
However, if you want to define the size of the swap partition yourself, you must create a corresponding partition.

4000 MB should be sufficient for swap on newer computers.

7.3.3. Advanced Features

Advanced features are explicitly not intended for the average user.
These are functions for advanced users.
Interested users will also get impressions of functions that are still in an experimental stage.

You can encrypt your system and use LVM, which is intended for advanced users.

The **ZFS** file system offers the possibility to make snapshots of the system, in addition to some other functions.
In doing so, the operating system can be reset to an old status in case problems occur after unsuccessful updates.

You can find ZFS in **Advanced Features.**

7.4. Set up the Time Zone

The hard disk is now partitioned and set up so that Ubuntu can be installed on it.

Before this can happen, however, some information is needed. For the clock in the computer to work properly, the **time zone** must be set up.

According to the information provided earlier Ubuntu will recognize where you are.

You can use the map to check if the localization has been correctly detected.

Of course, you can also change the time zone here manually. For example, you may speak German and use a German keyboard, but be in another country.

7.5. Personalisation

In the next step, personal data is requested.

Who are you?

Your name:	Joe
Your computer's name:	joe-VirtualBox
	The name it uses when it talks to other computers.
Pick a username:	joe
Choose a password:	●●●●● Short password
Confirm your password:	●●●●●
	○ Log in automatically
	● Require my password to log in
	☐ Use Active Directory
	You'll enter domain and other details in the next step.

Back   Continue

The name of the computer is especially important if you want your PC to be part of a network.

Assign a **password for** the selected user name. This will be necessary for all administrative tasks in the future.

If, in Ubuntu's opinion, the password is too weak for some reason (see "Short Password" above), you will be notified.

Only a green check shows that everything is allright.

You will need the password when you log in, if you chose **Require password to log in.**

If you do not want to log in with a password, simply select **Log in automatically**.

You can define further users at a later time, each with their own passwords.

7.6. The Installation

Now installation of **Ubuntu 22.04** begins.

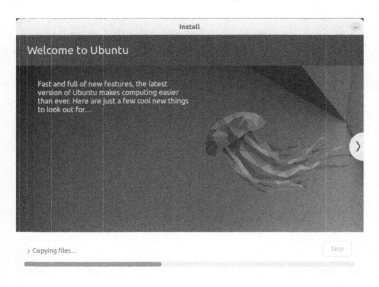

You can use the bar to keep track of how much time is still needed for the installation of **Ubuntu 22.04.**
To shorten the time, you will be shown basic information about **Ubuntu 22.04** in a slide show during the installation.

You have nothing more to do at the moment.
Just wait until the installation, which is fully automated from now on, has been completed.

7.7. First Start

You will be notified that the installation is complete.

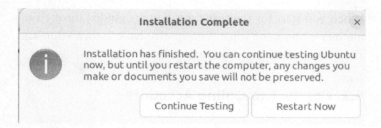

Now you have to **restart** the computer.

Please do not forget to remove the installation medium, otherwise you will end up back in the live system.

After restart the login screen will ask you for your password.

You can now log in with your password.

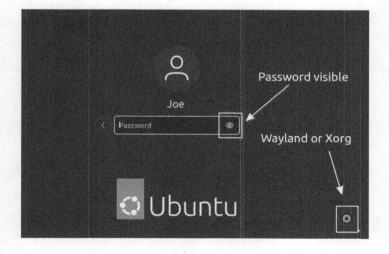

8. First Steps in Ubuntu 22.04

After a short time, the desktop interface of **Ubuntu 22.04** opens.

When you start for the first time, you are guided through some menu windows where you receive basic information and also have to make decisions on certain topics.

8.1. Connect to Online Accounts

At this point you will be asked if you want to connect immediately to online accounts that you may already have set up.

However, you can also log in to these accounts later.

If you do not have an account with these providers, **skip** the window.

You will find the corresponding button at the top right.

8.2. Ubuntu Data Collection

Ubuntu asks you whether you agree to certain user data being collected from you.

For the most part, these are details about your PC (memory, processor, graphics card, etc.).

Personal data is not collected at this point.

You can view the contents of the first report sent to **Canonical.**

To do this, press the button
View the first report.

Ubuntu's justification for collecting data is that it collects valuable information statistically, which benefits the user.

The default setting is:
Yes, send system info to Canonical
If you agree, confirm by clicking **Next**.

If not, select
No, don't send system info

You confirm your decision with **Next**.

8.3. Privacy

Here you set whether applications are allowed to determine your geographical location.

The Mozilla location service is used for this.

You can find out more about the details via the link **Privacy Policy.**

This function is switched off by default and must be explicitly activated by you.

If in doubt, don't change the setting.

This setting can be changed at any time at a later time.

You can find it under *Settings > Privacy*.

8.4. Ready to go

In the last window, you will be notified that you are ready to start and can immediately install further applications via the **Ubuntu Software** Center.

If you do not want to install any other applicationsnow, you can close the window with **Done**.

How to install applications with **Ubuntu software** is shown later in the book.

9. Software Updater

After a few minutes, Ubuntu may alert you that updated packages are available.

You will be asked if you want to install it.

You update your system with
Software Updater

You can decide whether you want to install the suggested updates immediately or whether you want to be reminded again
at a later time.

The update is done automatically by Ubuntu.

If you unfold **Details of Updates,** you can find out about de-
tails before you start the process by clicking **Install Now.**
You can exclude individual packages from the update.
However, I would only recommend this in exceptional cases.

10. The GNOME Desktop

After you have completed the initial setup, you can navigate the GNOME desktop and take first steps.
This chapter is for orientation.

10.1. The Dock

10.1.1. Preset

On the left side you will see a side bar which is called
Dock.

Ubuntu has its own version of the **Dash-to-Dock** extension installed by default.

The Dock offers you direct access to applications and other important functions of the operating system via buttons.

The dock can of course be configured to your own needs.

Thus, both the appearance and the content of the bar
can be changed.
How to do this is described in this chapter.

By default, the **side bar** (dock) looks like this:

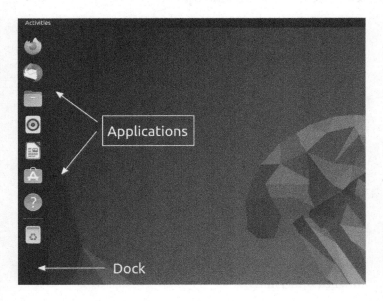

In the dock you will find starters for common applications.

- Internet browser Firefox
- E-mail client Thunderbird
- File manager Nautilus
- Music player Rhythmbox
- Word processing with LibreOffice Writer
- Ubuntu Software
- Help centre

Direct access to basic applications is made possible on this way.

At the very bottom left is the button with which you can open the **application overview.**

This button is called a **launcher**.

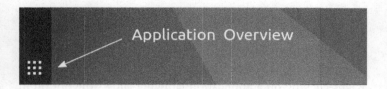
Application Overview

In addition, external devices are also displayed in the dock if they are connected.
These include external hard drives, SD cards, USB sticks or even ebook readers.

10.1.2. Configuration of the Dock

It is very likely that you will want to configure the dock according to your own preferences.
You can execute the most important actions directly from the interface.

10.1.3. Removing Application Launchers

If you have no use for certain programmes that are in the Dock, you can of course remove them.
All you have to do is to right-click on the corresponding application launcher.

In the pop-up menu you will now see the option
Remove from Favourites.
This way you remove the button you don't need.

10.1.4. Adding application launchers

If you want to add apllication starters to the dock, first open
the application overview.
All installed applications are displayed here.
Right-clicking on a application launcher shows the option in
the pop-up menu
Add to favourites.
This way you add the selected programme launcher to the
dock.
It is initially displayed in last position.

10.1.5. Order of Application Launchers

To change the order of the application launchers, press the
left mouse button and hold it while moving the button to the
position you want.

10.2. Applications Overview

In the **Application Overview,** all installed applications are shown in alphabetical order.
Click on the Launcher to open the **Applications Overview**.

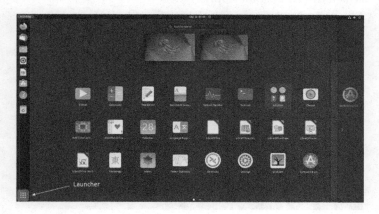

Unlike other desktop environments, applications in GNOME are not categorised.
For example, **Rhythmbox** is located right next to **Settings**.

Categories
You can group applications together in shared folders.
You create a new folder by dragging an application onto another application while holding down the left mouse button.
This automatically creates a new folder that you can name individually.

Example:
Drag the game **Mines** onto **Sudoku**. Give the resulting folder the name **Games**.

To find certain programmes more quickly, it is therefore a good idea to use the **search bar.**

This is located at the top centre of the window.

It is often enough to enter the first letters into the search bar. GNOME will then automatically find all applications to which this entry could apply.

For example, if you type the letters **f** and **i,** the Internet browser **Firefox** will be displayed.

If you have installed several applications that happen to begin with **f** and **i,** you will see all matches. By entering another letter, you narrow down the selection again.

In addition, depending on the configuration of the search bar, you may be shown further results.

For example, the search field can also be used as a calculator.

To do this, type a calculation task into the search bar.

The result will be displayed in the line below.

The integrated calculator is used for this.

You can also make general search queries here. For example, type the word **system**.

Ubuntu now assumes that you probably want to know something about the system and therefore offers you a link to the application **system monitor.**

If you type the word **game**, installed games will be displayed.

Since there is not enough space in the application overview to display all installed programmes, the content is spread over several pages.

You can select these conveniently using the round buttons at the bottom of the page.
However, these are quite small and inconspicuous.

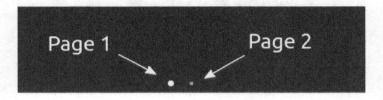

The filled dot indicates the currently selected page.

10.3. The Top Panel

The Top bar (panel) is divided into three sections.

- Activities
- Clock, calendar and notifications
- Status menu

10.3.1. Activities Overview

With **Activities** on the far left you can switch to the **Activities Overview**.

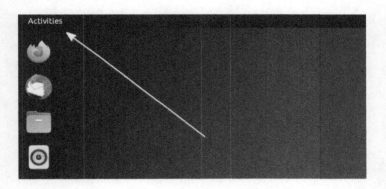

Activities Overview

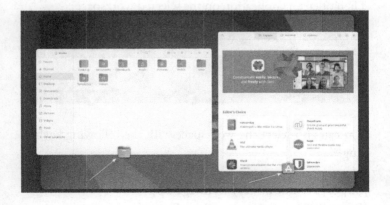

Alternatively, open **activities** with the **[Super key]** (also called Windows key).

This is located between **[Ctrl]** and **[Alt]** and often shows the Microsoft logo.

In overview mode you will also find the **search bar** and an overview of all activated **workspaces**.

10.3.2. Workspaces

You can create multple virtual workspaces in **Ubuntu 22.04** and switch between them very easily.

These are called **Workspaces**.

You can open a word processor on one desktop, an Internet browser on a second, and an image editing programme on a third.

Open the **Application Overview**.

You can see all workspaces right beneath the search bar.

Now select a workspace.

Then open an application on the selected workspace.

You can also select the workspace with the following keybinding:

[Super] (Windows key) + **[Image up]**
[Super] (Windows key) + **[Page Down]**

You can move content from one workspace to another by **holding down the left mouse button.**

In the example, an open **Ubuntu Software** window is dragged from **Desktop 2** to **Desktop 1.**

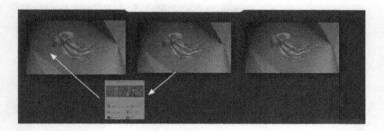

It is also possible to move individual windows using keyboard shortcuts.

[Shift] + [Super] + [Page Up] : Window is moved to workspace above the current one.

[Shift] + [Super] + [Page Down] : Window is moved to workspace below the current one.

10.3.3. Clock and Notifications

If you press the clock in the middle of the bar, a calendar will open.

In addition to the information on the current date, you will also find a **notification window** here.

You will be notified here about everything you have activated in the settings.

You will also be alerted here when updates are available for installation.

If you temporarily do not wish to receive notifications, switch this function off using **Do not disturb.**

10.3.4. Status Menu

On the far right is the **status menu**.

Here you can find setting options for frequently used functions.

- The volume control for the audio system
- Network connection and Bluetooth
- Battery indicator, if applicable
- Button to lock the PC
- Button for logging out, restarting and shutting down

Direct access to the **settings** is available via the cogwheel symbol.

10.4. Preinstalled Applications

The number of pre-installed applications depends on whether you selected the normal installation or the minimal installation during installation.
The applications listed in this book are automatically installed together with the operating system during normal installation. This is not the case with the minimal installation.

10.4.1. Office Applications

10.4.1.1. LibreOffice

LibreOffice is a complete office suite that is structured similarly to Microsoft Office.
The following individual applications are included:

- LibreOffice Writer
- LibreOffice Calc
- LibreOffice Impress
- LibreOffice Draw

These are a word processor, a spreadsheet program, a presentation program and a drawing programme.

Not included is communication software with the same functions as Outlook provides.

LibreOffice Writer is a word processing program.
It is comparable to Microsoft Word.

Just like the competitor product, you can use it to produce any type of text document.
Serial letters are just as feasable as longer texts with sophisticated formatting.
By default, the usual fonts **Arial** and **Times New Roman are** not delivered.
However, these can be installed after confirming the licence agreement.

```
apt install ttf-mscorefonts-installer
```

Writer can import and export files in Word format (.doc and .docx).

LibreOffice Calc is a spreadsheet application.
It is comparable to **Microsoft Excel**.

You can do all kinds of calculations with it.

In this way, budget books, financial planners and other calculations for private households can be created.

Calc could also be an alternative to Excel for small and medium-sized enterprises.

Files in Excel format (.xls and .xlsx) can be both imported and exported.

However, in some cases formatting problems can occur in direct exchange with Excel.

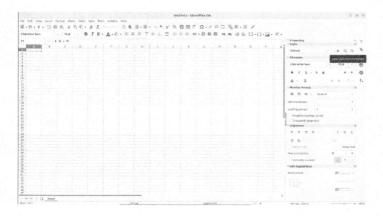

LibreOffice Impress is a presentation program.
It is comparable to **Microsoft PowerPoint**.

You can use it to design lectures.
Individual slides are combined as a **screen presentation.**

A wide range of design options are available.
You can design the individual slides freely or use one of the numerous templates that LibreOffice comes with as standard.

In addition, there is a wide range of presentation options to choose from.
It is also possible to use two or more displays.

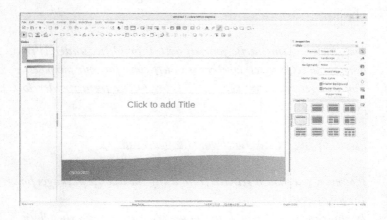

LibreOffice Draw

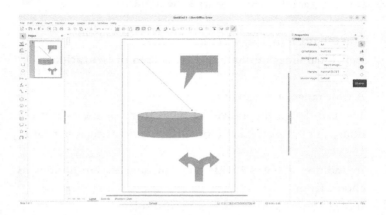

LibreOffice Draw can be used to design geometric drawing objects.

You can also familiarise yourself with LibreOffice under Windows or MacOS to test whether it is sufficient for your purposes. You can get the latest version of Libre Office from the developers' website.

https://de.libreoffice.org/download/download/

However, you should refrain from using the website packages for Linux as well.
In this case, it is always better to use the version from the Ubuntu repositories.
This is the only way to ensure that everything works smoothly.

10.4.1.2. Document Viewer

The **Document Viewer** is available for viewing PDF documents.

Documents with the extension .pdf are automatically opened with this application after a double click.

Individual pages can be viewed either continuously or double-sided.
However, editing PDFs is not possible with this program.
This requires specialised applications.

But a simple slide show is built in.

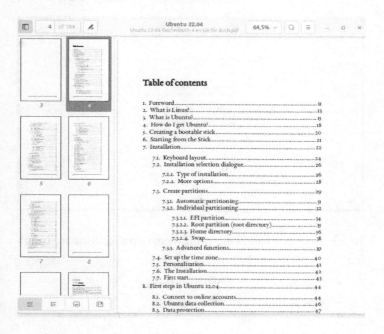

10.4.2. Multimedia

Rhythmbox

With **Rhythmbox,** individual playlists can be created.
Music data stored on the hard disk can be used for this purpose.
The operation is very intuitive and simple.
In addition, **Rhythmbox is** also suitable as a CD player.
An integrated radio player with countless pre-configured stations rounds off the picture.
However, **Rhythmbox is** not a multimedia player like VLC.

Videos can therefore not be played with it!

In addition, the following multimedia applications are installed:

- **Videos**   **Video player**
- **Cheese**   **Webcam**

10.4.3. Graphics Applications

Document Scanner

If your scanner is compatible with Linux, it will be detected automatically.
In some cases, however, it is necessary to download proprietary drivers from the manufacturer's website and install them by yourself.
Usually, instructions are provided that explain the individual steps in detail.

Document Scanner is a very simple program. However, it is good enough for simple scans.

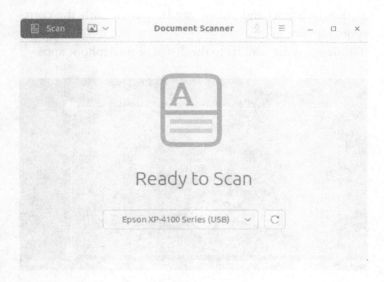

Screenshot

Screenshot makes it very easy to take screenshots of your screen. It is very intuitive.

With Screenshot it is possible,

- to take a screenshot of the entire content of the screen.
- to take a screenshot of the active window.
- to take a screenshot of any selected section.

In addition, you can also record short videos.

Both screenshots and videos can be started with the corresponding button.
The design is very similar to the design of smartphone apps.

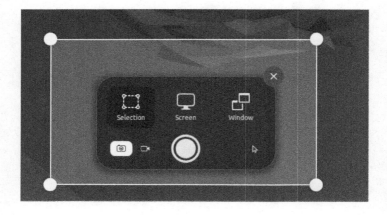

10.4.4. Internet

10.4.4.1. Thunderbird

Many users use their email provider's website to receive and send emails.

With **Thunderbird,** however, a program is available with which you can conveniently manage several mailboxes, even from different providers.

You may already know Thunderbird from Windows.

You can conveniently import your mailboxes that you have created under Windows to Linux.

If you have not used Thunderbird before, simply create a new account.

All you need is your e-mail address and the password.

10.4.4.2. Firefox

The **Firefox Internet Browser** is preinstalled.

However, this is a snap package.
Canonical has removed Firefox from the official repositories and now only offers this browser - just like Chromium - as a snap.
There are some disadvantages with snaps that I would like to point out here.
The start-up time of Firefox increases significantly.
Including an extension to download GNOME extensions directly from the homepage no longer works.
However, it is possible to remove the snap package and install a PPA of Firefox ESR instead.
This is a somewhat older version of Firefox, but it is carefully maintained. In Debian Stable, Firefox ESR is used as the default.
First, remove Firefox after you have saved the profile.

```
sudo snap remove firefox
```

Then you integrate the PPA.

```
sudo add-apt-repository ppa:mozillateam/ppa
&& sudo apt update
```

Then you install Firefox ESR.

```
sudo apt install firefox-esr firefox-esr-locale-en
```

On the Mozilla website you can also find a current version of Firefox, but you have to integrate it manually. Instructions for this are available.

10.4.5. Utilities

10.4.5.1. Passwords and Keys

Here you can lock up all the passwords and access codes you need, just like in a safe.

You gain access to all stored passwords through a single master password.

The master password is initially your personal password that you assigned during installation.

However, it is not advisable to use this password here.

Once someone knows this password, they have access to all passwords.

Therefore, one should generate another master password at this point, which is used exclusively to unlock access to the passwords contained in this program.

You define a new password via

Login > Right-click > Change Password.

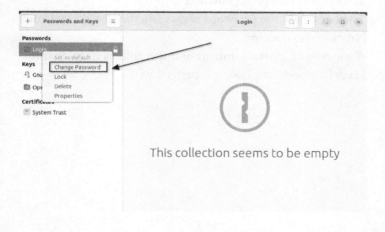

You lock and unlock access via the lock icon on the right-hand side.

You can add new passwords by pressing the + **key.**
Select what type of password it is.

In this example, I have added the access password for a fictitious e-mail account.
You can assign any name (description) for it.
Your password will be evaluated.
The bar below the password shows whether the desired combination is also secure.
A mixture of letters, numbers and special characters that makes as little sense as possible is preferable.

Do not forget to block access again afterwards (lock symbol)!

Unlocking requires legitimisation.
You will need the password you have just created.
After successful unlocking, you will see a list of all the entries you have saved.

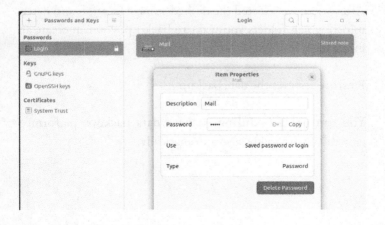

10.4.5.2. Backups

You open **Backups** in the Application Overview.

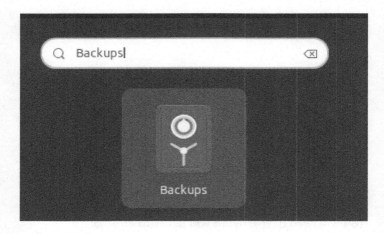

You will find everything you can configure here.

After you have selected the desired storage location and determined which folders you want to back up, you can create an initial backup.

Restore restores the data backup.

You can use **Scheduling** to have data backups performed either daily or weekly, also automatically.

You set up the data backup via **Create my first Backup**.
You define the folders to be backed up and the folders to be
ignored.

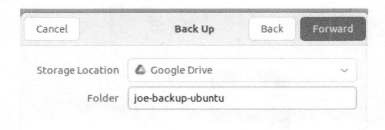

In the next step, you determine where the data backup is to be saved.

You can determine the backup location locally or externally. Google Drive would be an external location. However, it is also possible to store the data on an internal or external hard drive.

It is also possible to encrypt the backup with a password so that no one can access the data without knowing the password.

10.4.5.3. Text Editor Gedit

If you use Linux, you have a very wide selection of text editors.

Which one is right for you depends on the tasks you want to do with it.

Gedit is the default text editor in Ubuntu 22.04.

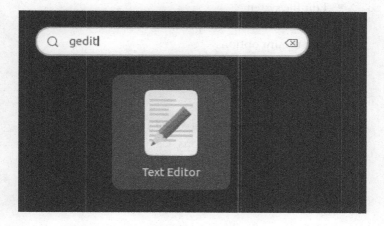

In the application overview you will also find the program if you are searching for Text Editor.

For simple configurations, **Gedit** is usually good enough.

You open **Gedit** via the application overview or via the terminal with the command gedit.

10.4.5.4. Disks

With **Disks** you can obtain information about all disks and drives in your system.
Furthermore, it is possible to edit partitions in many ways.

- Format partitions
- Edit partitions
- Edit file system
- Change the size of the partition
- Edit mount options
- Create partition image
- Check drives

You open the menu via the **cogwheel symbol**.
You can access further options via the **button with the three dots**.
Check the condition of the hard disk here with
SMART DATA and self-tests.

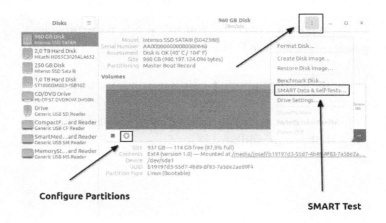

Configure Partitions

SMART Test

10.4.5.5. System Monitor

System Monitor shows you at a glance how busy your computer's hardware is.
This information is updated on an ongoing basis.

CPU shows the load on the processor. The individual cores are also taken into account separately.

Memory and Swap shows the usage of memory (RAM).

Network shows the load on the network. A distinction is made between sent and received data.

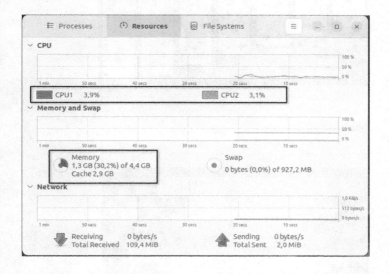

In addition, **Processes** can be used to obtain detailed information about what is currently keeping the system busy.

10.4.6. Games

Ubuntu 22.04 offers some simple games that are pre-installed.

Solitaire

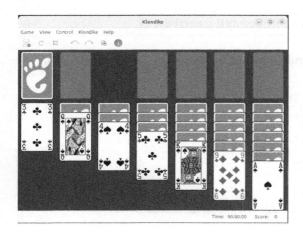

Mahjongg

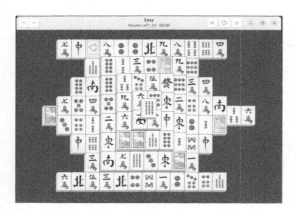

11. Software and Updates

You open this Application via the **application overview**.

11.1. Ubuntu Applications

You decide here whether you want to use only **open source** (free) software or also **proprietary** software.
Open source means that the source code of a program is openly accessible and may be changed.
On the other hand, there are applications where the source code is not open. This applies to almost all commercial programs.
(Microsoft, Apple, Adobe, etc.)

The following **repositories** are preset here :

- main   open source
- universe   open source
- restricted   not open source
- multiverse   not open source

As a rule, you do not have to change anything here, unless you want to use open source software exclusively.

However, you would then also exclude drivers and codecs that may be important for the smooth functioning of your operating system.

11.2. Updates

You determine here the way in which updates are to be made.

Automatically check for updates

You can choose:

- daily
- every two days
- weekly
- every two weeks
- never

You can specify whether security updates should be downloaded and installed automatically or only displayed.

Most users would like to stay with the chosen LTS variant of Ubuntu and not switch to one of the intermediate versions. Therefore, the default setting for notifications about new Ubuntu versions is that you are only notified about updates for **long-term support versions.**

The next LTS version is **Ubuntu 24.04**.
So you will not be informed about possible updates to 22.10, 23.04 or 23.10, as these are versions that are only supported for 9 months.
Should you nevertheless wish to change to such a version, select in this menu
For each new version.

11.3. Additional Drivers

Here you can, for example, install the proprietary driver of your graphics card if you are not satisfied with the open source one.

Standard tasks are no problem with the open source driver; for graphics-intensive applications, the proprietary driver is usually better suited.

Ubuntu shows you which alternative proprietary drivers are possible for your card.

All you have to do is select it and then press

Confirm **Apply Changes.**

The open source driver for your **Nouveau** graphics card is already pre-installed.

However, this can be replaced by the NVIDIA binary driver suggested and tested by Ubuntu.

Third-party drivers can also be used for WLAN cards and other hardware components.

It is definitely worth taking a look at the alternatives suggested by Ubuntu.

11.4. Livepatch

This tab is usually of little interest to home users.

Here you can set up a **Livepatch,** which makes it no longer necessary to restart the computer after kernel updates.
For this you need an Ubuntu Advantage subscription.
However, this is subject to a charge.

This function is only relevant for computers that are not to be switched off for a longer period of time.
This therefore is suitable for server applications where computers are in operation around the clock.
In this case, it makes sense not to interrupt the running operation by an update.

For many updates, however, a restart is not necessary anyway.
Furthermore, most private users switch off their computer at the end of the day.

12. Software Center (Ubuntu Software)

12.1. Installing Applications

It is very likely that you need additional software for your individual needs.

For example, applications for graphics editing or video editing are missing.

However, you can extend Ubuntu according to your wishes by installing applications later.

Unlike with Windows, in Linux you do not have to search the Internet for suitable programs. In fact, you should avoid doing so.
In the **repositories** (package sources) you will find basically everything that is available in Linux.

So you get everything from a single source and even free of charge in most cases.

By downloading your applications directly from the Ubuntu package sources, they are also more trustworthy than much of what you find on the Internet for Windows.

There are several ways to select and install applications.

The first and easiest way is via the **Ubuntu Software** which you will find in the Dock.
Ubuntu software is represented by a shopping bag .

Don't be put off by a shopping bag symbol.
You don't have to buy anything here.

After starting **Ubuntu software,** you will see an overview
that will make it easier for you to proceed.

In the upper section you will find recommendations from
Ubuntu (Editor's choice).

Further down, categories help you to search for specific programs.

Let's assume you would like to **edit** your **holiday photos** and are now looking for an appropriate program.

If you know what the application is called, you can search for it using the **magnifying glass** at the top left.

If you don't know the name, it's a good idea to look for it in the **Art and Design** category.
All the programs you will now be shown have more or less to do with graphics and photography.
To get more information about a specific application, click on the corresponding button.

Using **Darktable** as an example, I will show you how to install your chosen program.

Darktable is a very good photo editing programme that allows you to edit the brightness, contrast, saturation, exposure and many other properties of your image.

Many applications are displayed in different versions. In addition to packages from the Ubuntu repositories, **snaps** are also available for selection.
This is also the case with **Darktable.**

After you have decided which version of **Darktable** you want to install and pressed the appropriate button, a window will open showing you a brief description of the application and a view of the program interface.

In addition, you will receive information on the current version and which source is used for the download.

For opinions and comments, see the reviews below.

If you have decided to install this application, you only have to press the corresponding **Install** button.

In the following window you will be informed that you must enter your password for the installation. This is the password you entered during installation and which you also need to log in.

This prevents software from being installed on your computer without your knowledge and is an important security measure.

You can now follow the progress of the installation with the help of a bar and the corresponding percentage display.

The installation process usually does not take very long.

12.2. Remove Applications

However, via **Ubuntu software** you can not only install applications, but also remove them if you do not like them.

To do this, select the **Installed** button in the top centre of **Ubuntu Software**.

The following window will show you all the applications that are currently installed on your computer.
Next to it you will see the button labelled **Remove.**

However, please be careful and under no circumstances delete applications of which you do not know exactly what function they have.
In the worst case, deleting important system programs can make the entire operating system unusable.

For information on how to install and remove applications in the **terminal,** please refer to the corresponding chapter.

13. Snap Store

Snaps are an alternative and new type of program package.
Snaps are cross-platform, unlike the traditional apps you get from the Ubuntu repos.
Snaps also allow you to get updated versions of applications faster, because they also install the dependencies that may be missing on your system.

For many applications, in Ubuntu software you will find an older version from the repositories and a newer one in snap format.
You can decide for yourself which version you want to use.
You can also use both at the same time.
However, please bear in mind that a Snap version requires significantly more storage space on your hard disk than the conventional version.
It is also possible that the theme (appearance) you have chosen is not supported.

The basic package **snapd** is already pre-installed with Ubuntu.

Search for available packages via the **snapcraft.io** website.
You then install the desired application via the terminal.

```
snap install package name
```

A list of all installed snap packages can be obtained with the following command:

```
snap list
```

```
Name                      Version          Rev    Tracking          Publisher   Notes
bare                      1.0              5      latest/stable     canonical   base
core20                    20220826         1623   latest/stable     canonical   base
firefox         ←         105.0.2-1        1918   latest/stable/... mozilla     -
gnome-3-38-2004           0+git.6f39565    119    latest/stable/... canonical   -
gtk-common-themes         0.1-81-g442e511  1535   latest/stable/... canonical   -
snap-store                41.3-64-g512c0ff 599    latest/stable/... canonical   -
snapd                     2.57.2           17029  latest/stable     canonical   snapd
snapd-desktop-integration 0.1              14     latest/stable/... canonical   -
```

In the example, Firefox is installed as a snap.
The Snap Store, which is the basis of Ubuntu software, is also a snap.

Updates of all installed snap packages are done with the following command:

```
snap refresh
```

If you only want to know which snap packages have updates available, you can display a list with the following command:

```
snap refresh --list
```

If you only want to update a specific snap package, you can do so with the following command:

```
snap refresh package name
```

14. Flatpaks

Flatpaks offer another way of installing newer versions of applications on your computer independently of the chosen distribution and its package management.

Flatpaks provide both the application itself and the required dependencies in a self-contained package.

To use Flatpaks, first install the basic package in the terminal.

```
apt install flatpak
```

Then include the Flatpak repository.

```
flatpak remote-add --if-not-exists flathub
https://flathub.org/repo/flathub.flatpakre-
po
```

For the changes made to take effect, restart the computer.

You can install applications with

```
apt flatpak install package name
```

If you want to have an overview of which flatpaks are installed on your system, you can find out with the following command:

```
flatpak list
```

The displayed list shows the name of the application, a short description, the version number and also the source.

You update Flatpaks with the following command:

```
sudo flatpak update package name
```

If you want to update all installed flatpaks, use this command:

```
sudo flatpak update --user
```

Configuration data for Flatpaks can be found at the following address:

/home/user/.var/app/

Example:

The full path for the **Franz** application is:
/home/user/.var/app/com.meetfranz.Franz/config

__Franz__ is a chat and messaging application.
Suitable for the integration of Twitter, Telegram, Discord and many other such services.

15. PPA (Personal Package Archive)

At the moment of the release of Ubuntu 22.04, all applications included in the package sources are relatively up-to-date.
Ubuntu 22 .04 is supported for a total of 5 years.
During this time, new versions of many programs will be available, but they do not find their way into the Ubuntu repositories.
Therefore, after a certain time, the desire to update applications such as Libre Office or GIMP may arise.
One possible way to do this is via Personal Package Archive (PPA).
To be able to install these applications, you must add the necessary package source.
This is basically done with the following command:

```
sudo apt-add-repository ppa:USER/user-ppa
```

An update of the package sources is done by

```
sudo apt update
```

You can then install the application.

```
sudo apt install package name
```

Example: GIMP PPA

```
sudo add-apt-repository ppa:savoury1/gimp -y
sudo apt update
sudo apt install gimp
```

You can find the respective names for the package source by searching the Internet.

16. Alternative Installation Options

However, **Ubuntu software** is not the only way you can install applications.

Alternatives are:

- **Synaptic**
  For experienced users, this programme offers a considerably wider range of functions than Ubuntu software.
  However, it requires a steeper learning curve to be able to exploit all the possibilities.

- **The Terminal**
  All applications in the Ubuntu Repositories can also be installed via the terminal.
  However, the prerequisite is that you know the exact name of the programme in question or know how to find it out.

No snaps or flatpaks can be installed via Synaptic.
On the other hand, you have access to all the applications in the Ubuntu repositories.

The installation of snaps and flatpaks, on the other hand, is possible without any problems via the command line.

16.1. Synaptic Package Manager

Via **Ubuntu software** or the **terminal,** install the **application**
Synaptic Package Manager.

Open **Synaptic** via the application overview.

You will need your personal password for this because **Synaptic** allows you to make changes to your system.

Click on the **Search** button (magnifying glass at the top right) to open a window.
Here you type in the name of the desired programme. (In the example darktable).
Confirm with **Search**.

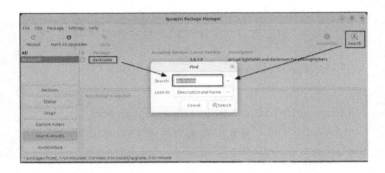

In the main window you will now see a selection of applications that contain the term **darktable** in their names.
See the description for more information on the packages found.

In this case, you will find the program itself in the first line of the main window.

However, with other applications there are also extensions and additional programmes that are eligible for installation. Therefore, read the description of the packages carefully.

Install the program by ticking the checkbox to the left of the program name.

Confirm **Mark for installation**.

In addition to installing the program, additional packages usually have to be installed.

These are mostly dependencies that the program needs but are not yet on the computer.

Without these necessary changes, the application will not work.

Confirm with **Mark**.

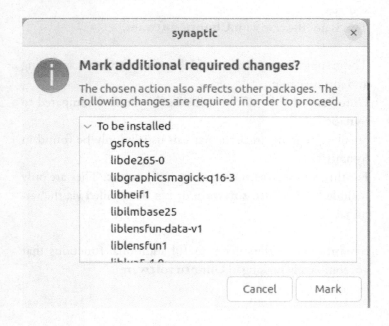

You can mark several applications and install them together later.

By **applying,** the application and the required packages are finally installed.

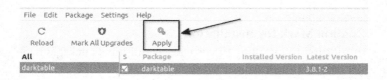

You may ask yourself why use **Synaptic** when there is **Ubuntu software** available.
The advantage of **Synaptic** is that with this application you can find everything that is included in the Ubuntu package sources.
This is not the case with **Ubuntu software.**

The graphical user interface of **Ubuntu software** is appealing and intuitive to use.
Unfortunately, the offer is considerably limited compared to **Synaptic.**
Smaller programs in particular can usually only be found in **Synaptic**.
For this, you won't find any snaps in **Synaptic.** They are only included in **Ubuntu software** or can be installed via the terminal.

Synaptic also offers many useful additional functions that are completely missing in **Ubuntu software.**

16.2. Terminal

Via the terminal, you can easily install and also remove any application that is in the activated repositories.
To do this, open the terminal.

```
sudo apt install package name
```

The prerequisite for this is that you know what name the program has.
This is sometimes complicated by the fact that desktop environments no longer display the correct name.
For example, on the GNOME Desktop you will find theprogram **Text Editor**, although it is actually the **application Gedit**.

Any attempt to install this programme with the command *apt install text editor* would fail.

Only with *apt install gedit* you install **Gedit**, which will be shown to you later as **Text Editor.**

This might be a little bit confusing, but it's the way that it is.

17. The File Manager (Nautilus)

17.1. Overview

The **File Manager** gives you easy access to the important places in your system.

In the **File Manager** you can

- View folders and files
- Create folders and files
- Move folders and files
- Copy folders and files
- Delete folders and files

From here you also have access to the file system.
System configurations are usually done in the terminal or via an editor, but the file manager is usually a good place to get an overview.
The different desktop environments usually have their own file managers.
For Ubuntu using the Gnome desktop, this is **Nautilus**.
The variety of functions is somewhat limited compared to other file managers, but should be good enough for most everyday tasks.

Familiarise yourself with this tool, because you will certainly use it a lot in the future.

You open **Nautilus** via the Dock by clicking the files icon.

This is what the file manager looks like:

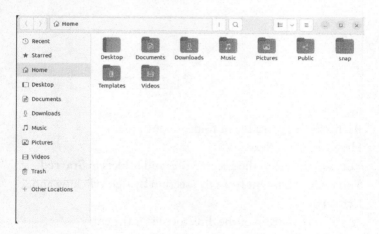

On the left side there is a list of selectable **directories**.
This area is called the **sidebar.**
By default, the **home folder** is selected here.

However, you also have direct access to the directories **pictures**, **documents**, **downloads**, **music** and **videos**.
In addition, the contents of the **trash folder** can be selected here.

Via **Recent** you have access to the files you opened recently.

Use **Starred** to quickly navigate to folders and files you have previously marked.

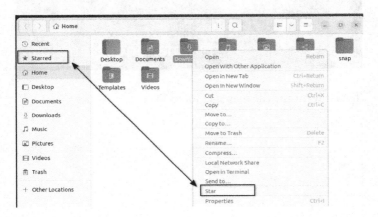

Right-clicking on a file or folder opens a menu.
Here you select **Star**.
You will then find the selected files and folders in **Starred**.
You remove content from this section by right-clicking and se-
lect **unstar**.
At the very bottom of the directory list is the entry
Other Locations.
This leads you

- to the file system (called **computer** here)
- to the established networks
- to additional hard disks (internal or external)
- to USB sticks
- to SD cards

In the main window you can see which contents are in the currently opened directory.

In the **personal folder (home folder)** you can see all the directories that were either created by the operating system during the installation or by yourself at a later time.

Pictures
Image files are stored in this directory.

Documents
Documents of all kinds are stored in this directory. For example, text files or spreadsheets that you create with Libre Office can be found here.

Downloads
All files that you download from the Internet can be found in this directory.

Music
Find your music collection here.

Public
In this directory you can collect files that you want to make publicly accessible in a network.

Snap
This folder contains files that are necessary for the proper functioning of Snaps.

Videos

Since there are now many useful applications for video editing, it also makes sense to create a directory for video files in the personal folder.

Videos that you may download from the Internet (please observe copyright) will end up in the Downloads folder first, but you can move them to this place at a later time.

Templates

In this folder you can store all the templates for various applications that already exist or that you have created. This way you do not have to search for them for a long time after starting the corresponding program.

Desktop

Every file you place on the desktop can be found in this folder.

A folder is placed on the desktop by copying or moving it to the **Desktop** directory.

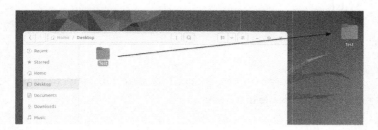

17.2. Configuration of the Home Folder

Of course, you can also design the contents of your personal folder in a completely different way.

17.2.1. Overview

You can:

- Create additional folders
- Create subdirectories
- Delete existing folder
- Rename existing folder

Double-click on a directory to display its contents.
These can be individual files or also further folders.

The arrows in the top left corner help you navigate.
The right arrow opens the selected directory, the left arrow leads you back to the starting point.

At the top of the directory list is the entry
Recent.
Files that you have used recently are stored here.
Right-clicking on a directory opens up numerous possibilities for further editing.

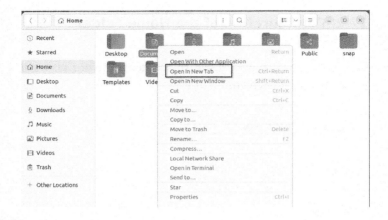

You can create a directory

- Open - the selected directory is opened in the current window and replaces the previously opened one.
- Open in new tab - a new tab is created for the new directory.
- Open in new window - a new window is opened additionally for the new directory.

Example:

The directory **Documents** has been opened in a new tab.
In this way, you can select any number of open directories via the corresponding tabs.

You can **move** or **copy** a directory or a file.

After right-clicking on the directory or the file

- select **Cut** if you want to move the file.
- select **Copy** if you want to copy the file.

The file will be saved to a clipboard.
Now change to the target directory.
With **Paste** (right-click on empty space in the target folder) you execte the process
However, you can also move the directory with the commands **Move to ...** and **Copy to ...** to move or copy the directory to another location.
In this case, you must specify a **destination** and confirm the operation with **Select.**

You can **delete** directories and files by moving the selected directory to the **trash**.
However, this action does not delete it permanently.
You can find and restore the file inside the trash at any time.
Only when you click **empty trash** the deletion process will be carried out definitively.

With **Rename** it is possible to change the name of a file or directory.

In **Properties** you can view or change the **permissions** of the selected directory.
Here you can specify who else other than you should have full access to the directory.

17.2.2. Create a new Folder

Right click on the free space in the directory to open another pop-up menu.
Here you will find
New folder

Folder is Empty

When you click on it, a field with a blank line opens immediately.
Here you enter the name you have intended for the new folder.
The folder is then created by pressing **Enter** or the **Create** button.
If you change your mind, you can also cancel this action at any time. The corresponding button is located on the left side.

You can delete or rename the folder you have just created at any time.

17.2.3. Hiding the directory list

Press the **[F9]** key to show or hide the directory list. This gives you even more space for the contents.

17.2.4. Enlarge the Icons

With **[Ctrl] + [+] you** can enlarge Icons for the folders.
Press **[Ctrl] + [-] to** reduce the size of the Icons again.

You can also change the size of the icons permanently.
You will find the option for individual configuration in the file manager settings.

17.2.5. Create Bookmarks

You may want to pin your own directories or files in the directory list as a shortcut.

Example:
To do this, create a new file.txt called **Test** within the **Documents folder**.
Then drag it into the **directory list > New Bookmark** with the left mouse button pressed.

Right-clicking on this folder (in the directory list) opens a drop-down menu that offers you, among other things, to remove the entry again.

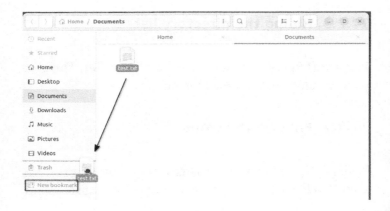

17.2.6. Show hidden Files

Hidden files are files or even folders that are not visible by default.

The simple reason for this is that they are thus protected from unauthorised or unqualified access.

Important configuration data is located here and should not be deleted lightly.

Thus, your personal settings from various applications are stored in this location.

The thunderbird folder is also located here.

These directories and files are marked with a dot in front of the file name.

For example, the corresponding Thunderbird folder looks like this:

.thunderbird

If for some reason you want to have access to the hidden files, use a keyboard shortcut.

[Ctrl] + [H] makes all invisible files and directories visible. You can also make the invisible folders visible via the menu (see picture on page 110!).

> Show hidden files

17.2.7. File Manager Settings

The appearance and behaviour of the file manager can be configured in many ways.

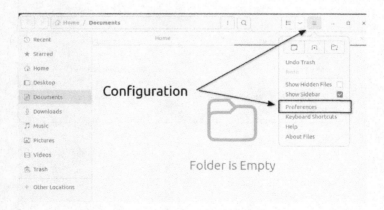

In **Settings** you will find many options for customising the file manager.

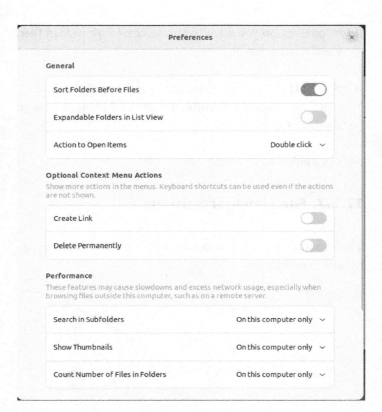

Preferences ✕

General

Sort Folders Before Files

Expandable Folders in List View

Action to Open Items   Double click ⌄

Optional Context Menu Actions

Show more actions in the menus. Keyboard shortcuts can be used even if the actions are not shown.

Create Link

Delete Permanently

Performance

These features may cause slowdowns and excess network usage, especially when browsing files outside this computer, such as on a remote server.

Search in Subfolders   On this computer only ⌄

Show Thumbnails   On this computer only ⌄

Count Number of Files in Folders   On this computer only ⌄

18. Settings

You won't find quite as many ways to customise your system to your liking in the Ubuntu Gnome interface as with some other desktop environments.

Nevertheless, various interesting configuration options await in the Settings section.

> *If this is not enough for you, you can load numerous other useful additions via the **GNOME** Tweak **tool** (Gnome Optimisations).*

But first we turn to the settings menu, which you will find by default.

To do this, go to the **application overview** and open **Settings**.

The following overview opens:

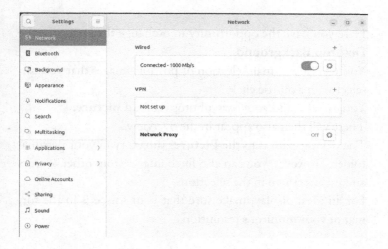

18.1. Network

Here you set up your network.

The wired connection is automatically detected by Ubuntu during installation.

The WLAN is also usually recognised, but you need your WLAN password to access it.

You can also set up VPN (virtual private network) or a network proxy here.

18.2. Bluetooth

Here you can configure your Bluetooth access.

18.3. Background

Here you have the opportunity to exchange the image for the **Desktop Background.**

You will find a small selection of possible images that you can select with a mouse click.

You can also add your own photos via **Add picture.**

These will then also appear in the overview.

The default path is to the **Pictures** directory in your personal folder. However, you can also fetch images from other sources and include them in the selection.

For an ideal display, make sure that your image is in the format of your monitor's resolution.

18.4. Appearance

18.4.1. Style and Accent Colors

You choose between **two settings** here.

- **Light**: Light background with light title bar
- **Dark**: Dark background with dark title bar

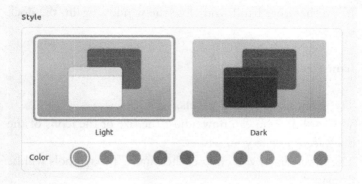

You can define the accent colors via **Color.**
This allows you to set the color of the folders.

You cannot change the system theme here.
You have to use GNOME-Tweaks for this.
The extension **User-Themes** can be used to install themes
that can be found in the Ubuntu repositories.

Not all themes work as good as the default!

18.4.2. Dock

Auto-hide the dock

You will find a switcher here that is set to **Off** by default.
The Dock always remains visible with this setting.
If you set this switch to **ON**, the dock is always hidden when windows overlap with it.
This means that a maximised window in this case fills the whole screen and the dock is hidden.
If, on the other hand, you close the window again, the dock reappears.

Icon Size

The default setting is **48 pixels**.
With a slider you can now adjust the size of the icons of the dock according to your wishes.
The fewer pixels you choose, the smaller the symbols will be displayed.
However, the change does not only affect the icons themselves. The width of the dock is also adjusted automatically.

Position on screen

You may not like the fact that the dock is on the left side of your screen.
The dock can also be placed at the **bottom** or on the **right**.

18.5. Notifications

By default, your system provides you with up-to-date information of all kinds.

One of the most important **notifications** is the information that system updates are available.

You can also switch off **notifications** completely.

In the corresponding menu you will see two buttons at the top.

Do not disturb: Here you can allow or disallow notifications.

Lock Screen Notifications: Here you can allow or disallow notifications on the lock screen.

In addition, you can also configure the notification function in detail for various applications.

To do this, simply click **ON** for one of the applications listed below.

A new window opens listing various options.

For example, you can switch on and off printer notifications.

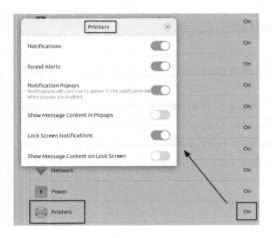

18.6. Search

Ubuntu 22.04 has a powerful search function. You can reach the search bar via **Activities.**

In **Settings** you can specify in which categories Ubuntu should search when you start a query.

You can also change the order of the search results.

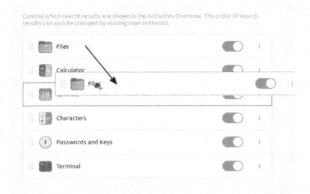

18.7. Applications

Here you will find default settings for all installed applications.
You can change these settings here.

Since access permissions are sometimes restricted for snap packages, you can make some changes here.

Example:
personal-files: allows access to personal files or directories

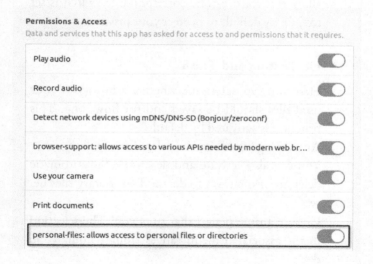

18.8. Privacy

The settings include the following items:

- **Connectivity**

  This function is intended to detect possible network problems.

- **Location services**

  These services allow applications to detect your geographical location. However, you must explicitly allow this feature. The corresponding switch is set to OFF by default to protect your privacy!

- **File History and Trash**

  Here you can determine whether a history of your used files should be saved and for how long. This function is activated by default.
  An existing history can be deleted at any time.
  You can also activate and deactivate the automatic deletion of the trash folder and temporary files here.
  Choose a time period that suits you! The selection in the associated menu ranges from 1 hour to 30 days.

- **Screen**

  You can have the screen locked automatically as long as you are not present. You regulate this with the corresponding switch button. In addition, you can also determine after what period of inactivity the screen is switched off.

- **Diagnostics**

  If you want to send bug reports to Canonical, activate this function.
  You can determine whether this should happen automatically or whether you want to be asked beforehand.

18.9. Online Accounts

Connecting to different **online accounts** is no problem in Ubuntu.
To do this, connect to the selected online service by entering your access data.
Various services are available for selection.

18.10. Sharing

With this function, you allow remote users to view and control your screen.

This can be useful if you have your computer serviced.
Normally, however, the switch is in the OFF position.

18.11. Sound

This is theer for your audio configuration.

System volume

At the very top you will find the fader for the **output volume** of your audio applications.

This setting affects all audio signals.

You can adjust the volume to over 100% by using the **over-amplfication** slider. However, this can lead to distortions.

It is therefore better to leave the slider in the OFF position.

Preferably, regulate signals that are too quiet in the respective application or via **Pavucontrol**.

Output

Here you set the output assignment for audio signals. This can be an internal sound generator, but also an external device that you have connected via a socket.

Ubuntu usually recognises which options are available to you.

Input

Here you set the input channel for audio recording.

This applies, if you want to make voice recordings via a connected microphone.

When your microphone has been correctly recognised, adjust the **recording volume** using the **Volume** indicator. Pay attention to possible distortion.

You can switch **warning tones** on and off and also adjust the volume via **system sounds.**

They are intended to support notifications.

18.12. Power

Power Mode
Affects system performance and power usage.

⊙ **Balanced**
Standard performance and power usage.

○ **Power Saver**
Reduced performance and power usage.

Power Saving Options

Screen Blank
Turns the screen off after a period of inactivity.   5 minutes ∨

Automatic Suspend
Pauses the computer after a period of inactivity.   Off

Power Mode

In most cases you better use **Balanced**. This is also default.
But if you want to reduce power usage, you can check the
Power Saver Option.

Power Saving Options

The screen is switched off after a set period of inactivity. The
shortest interval is 5 minutes.
In addition, you can decide whether the computer should go
into standby mode when it is inactive.

18.13. Display

Display

Ubuntu usually detects the **resolution** of your monitor automatically. However, you can change this at any time.

Scale allows you to enlarge the content of the screen.
You can choose between 100% (default), 125%, 150%, 175% .
Fractional scaling must be activated for this.
This can increase power usage, decrease speed and reduce display sharpness!

Night Light

Night Light displays the screen in warmer colours. This serves to be easier on the eyes.

Sunset to Sunrise:
This mode is automatically regulated by the time zone you have selected.

Times:
You can set an individual time from when the night mode should be active and for how long.

In addition, you can set a **Color Temperature** that is comfortable for you.

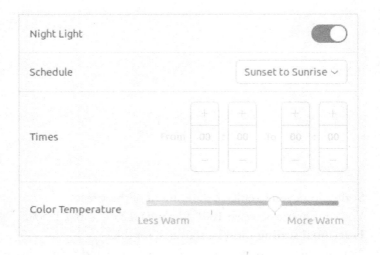

18.14. Mouse and Touchpad

Here you can change some basic settings that affect the behaviour of your mouse.

Primary Button
Left-handers can swap the right and the left mouse button here.
Mouse
Here you can adjust the mouse speed with a slider to your needs.
Natural Scrolling
This reverses the scroll direction when scrolling with the middle wheel of the mouse.
The default direction is reversed if you set the button to ON.

18.15. Keyboard

In this menu you will find the predefined keyboard shortcuts.

Example:

View and customize Shortcuts > Windows > Maximize Window:

[Super] + [Arrow up]

This means that you have to press these two buttons **simultaneously** to maximise the currently open and active window.

If you want to reset the window to its original size, press

[Super] + [Down Arrow]

You can set up individual keyboard shortcuts.
To do this, just double-click on a disabled function in the list.
Then you enter the desired keyboard shortcut.

18.16. Printer

In the best case, the printer is recognised automatically and you do not have to set anything up yourself.
If you want to add a printer, press the corresponding button and make sure that the printer is connected and switched on.

Ubuntu will then guide you through the necessary steps.

18.17. Removable Media

This menu gives you the option of specifying what should happen when inserting different removable media.
The default setting is to **ask what to do.**
However, you probably want an inserted audio CD, for example, to always start and play with the same program.
You can select your preferred application here.
Ubuntu will make suggestions as to which installed program might be suitable for the selected media.
However, you can select **another application.**

Select how media should be handled

CD audio	Ask what to do
DVD video	Ask what to do
Music player	Ask what to do
Photos	Ask what to do
Software	Run Software

Other Media...

☐ Never prompt or start programs on media insertion

In addition to the media listed here, you will find more options under **Other media.**

This way you can also set the corresponding programs for Blue-Ray media or e-book readers.

18.18. Region and Language

Normally, the language settings are already set up according to your specifications during the installation.

If you want to change this, it is possible in this menu.

18.19. Accessibility

Here you can set a higher contrast or change the size of the mouse cursor.
Text input can also be done with an on-screen keyboard and **AccessX** provides a comprehensive typing assistant.

You can add an **accessibility menu** permanently displayed in the top bar.
By default, the **accessibility menu** is switched off.

Switch it on!

A small icon (little man) then appears in the top panel, which opens a menu containing the most important configuration options.

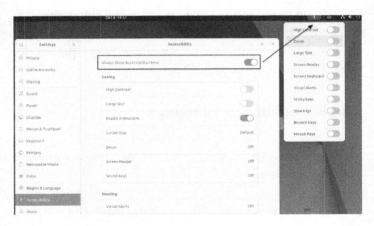

18.20. Users

Here you can change all the personal details you entered during installation.
To be able to make changes, unlock the settings with your password!

Here you can

- **Change the user name**

  To do this, enter the new user name.

- **Upload a picture (Avatar)**

  Ubuntu offers a selection of images.
  However, you can also upload your own image.

- **Change the password**

  To do this, you must first enter the currrent password. In the next line, enter the new password. Ubuntu gives you instructions on how to create a password that is as secure as possible.
  With **Change** you confirm the decision you have made.
  With **Cancel** you don't change the password.

- **Activate the automatic login**

  This is set as you selected it during installation.

- **Check the account activity**
  Here you can check all logins into your system.

18.21. About

Here you will find general information about

- the computer name you have chosen
- The installed memory
- the processor of your computer
- Graphics
- the GNOME version
- the type of operating system
- the diskon which Ubuntu is installed.

You can also check for updates here.
Press **Software Updates** !

18.22. Default Applications

Here you specify which installed applications should be used for certain tasks by default.

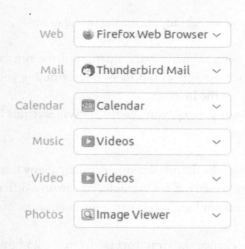

If you install several web browsers, you can specify here which one will be started when you open a link from outside (e.g. link in e-mail).

These presets are especially important if you have installed several different applications that all have the same or a similar function.

Clicking on a photo will automatically open the program you set here.

Depending on whether you want to view pictures only or edit them immediately, you make the appropriate selection here.

18.23. Date and Time

Normally, the date and also the time are automatically determined by the system according to the time zone you have selected.

The **time zone** was already set during installation.

The button for automatic determination of the time zone is set to OFF because this would require determining your current location via the Internet.
To protect your privacy, you should always leave this button in this position.

You can change the default settings manually at any time.
This may be necessary if, for example, you are in a different time zone but do not have access to the internet.

You can also change the **time format** from the 24-hour cycle to 12 hours (AM/PM).

19. GNOME Tweaks

An extension that is available in the Software Center
allows you to configure your system much more than
with **Settings**.

Open Ubuntu software and type tweaks in the search
bar.

This application is also called GNOME Tweak Tool
and allows you to customize advanced GNOME settings.

The next step is to install this program.

When the installation process is finished, you will
find it in the application menu.

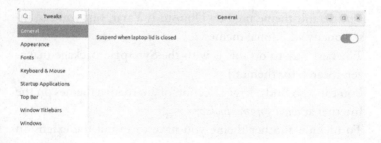

Tweaks is structured similarly to **Settings**.

On the left side you will find different categories, on the right
side in the main window the corresponding configuration options.

General you can switch the power saving mode on and off
for laptops with the lid closed.

19.1. Appearance

Here you can change the **appearance of** the distribution.

It is therefore important to remember the default settings so that you can always return to the original state if you do not like the new settings.

Here you can

- Exchange Icons
- Change design of the cursor
- Change Theme

The default theme used by Ubuntu is **Yaru,** but you can install many additional themes.
The best way to do this is with the **Synaptic** package manager. (Search for themes!)
You can also find a large selection of alternative themes on the Internet at *www.gnome-look.org* .
To include another theme you have to install the extension **user-themes**.
Only then does the additional theme appear in **Shell**.
As already mentioned, changing to a different theme affects the whole system.
This affects the file manager, the configuration menus but also most applications.
If you choose a dark theme, all backgrounds will be dark.

Please bear in mind that not every external theme integrates perfectly with Ubuntu 22.04!

19.2. Windows

Here you can adjust the behaviour of the windows to your needs.

Modal dialogs

Dialog windows cannot be moved separately.

Window Focus

The configuration of **Window Focus** determines,

- whether a window is to be activated by clicking with the mouse (clicking to focus)
- whether a window is to be activated by hovering over it with the mouse pointer (focus on hover)
- whether a window is to be activated by hovering over it with the mouse pointer and lose focus again when the pointer moves over the desk. (secondary click)

19.3. Windows Titlebars

Titlebar Actions determines what should happen when you double-click, middle-click or secondary-click (right mouse button) with your mouse on the bar.

For example, a double click can cause,

- that the window is maximised to screen size. (toggle maximize)
- that the window is minimized and thus disappears. (minimize)

19.3.1. Titlebar Buttons

If you do not like that the buttons of the title bar for closing, minimizing and maximising are on the right-hand side, you can move them to the left-hand side by placing them using the selection button (left/right).

In addition, you can delete both the maximise and minimise buttons from the bar completely by simply moving the slider to OFF.

19.4. Top Bar

Here you can activate or deactivate some additional functions for the top bar.

This is controlled by ON/OFF-Buttons.

You can hide the application menu, which shows the currently open applications in the upper bar.

If you are using your computer with a battery, you can display the remaining percentage of the battery charge.
In addition to the time in the middle of the bar, you can also display the date.
You can add the week numbers to your calendar.

19.5. Fonts

If you do not like the fonts used and the size you can change the font settings here.

The window title preset for the fonts:
- Ubuntu Regular   Font
- 11   Font size

Remember the default settings and try out different options in this menu until you like the selection you have made.

Confirm changes with the green **Select** button.

You should not change **Hinting** and **Antialiasing**, as optimal values are usually set here.

The **scaling factor** is a powerful tool.

The default setting is **1,00**.

You can scale up or scale down the screen content by changing this value.

19.6. Startup Applications

Specify here which applications should start automatically each time the operating system is started.

Pressing the **plus key (+)** shows you all the programmes that can be selected for an automatic start.

If you select **Firefox** the browser will start automatically after each login.

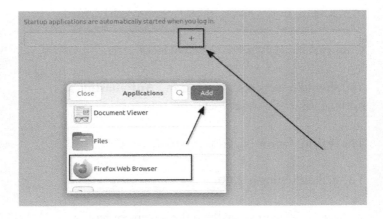

The selection can be undone by pressing **Remove**.

19.7. Keyboard and Mouse

Here you can set some very specific configurations for the behaviour of the mouse and keyboard.

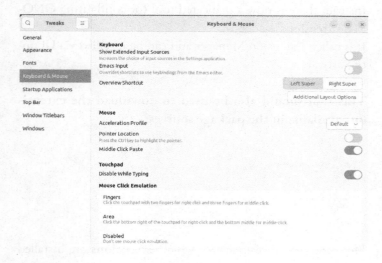

Keyboard

- Emacs Input
- Overview Shortcut

Mouse:

- Acceleration Profile
- Pointer Location
- Middle Click Paste
- Disable Touchpad while typing
- Mouse Click Emulation

20. Extensions

Since Ubuntu 22.04, access to extensions is no longer included in GNOME Tweaks.
Instead, there is now a dedicated tool for configuring GNOME Extensions.
It is called Extension Manager and can be installed via Ubuntu Software.

This tool should also be used to download the extensions available in the package sources.

Here you get an overview of which **extensions** are installed and which of them are activated.

The slider shows you the current status.

Gnome **Extensions** add more functions to your system.
You can decide for yourself whether you need the functions offered or not.

However, you will not find most of the available extensions in the installed system. They are also not an official part of Ubuntu.

You can get an overview on the GNOME website.

https://extensions.gnome.org

Here you will find a huge selection of extensions.
However, bear in mind that this is third-party software.
A proper integration into the system is usually given, but problems sometimes occur with Updates.
It is essential that the extension is compatible with the GNOME version used.

There are several **alternative ways** to install additional extensions.

20.1.1. Extensions via browser add-on

You can download the extensions directly from the website.

At the moment this procedure does not work with the Firefox version supplied, as it is a snap package.
It is therefore advisable to install Firefox-ESR as a PPA if you want to download extension on this way.

First you need to add the **GNOME Shell Integration** add-on to your browser.
In Firefox, click on the button with the three dashes at the top right.
In the menu you will find the item **Add-ons**.
Here you can search for GNOME Shell Integration.

In the terminal install:

```
sudo apt install chrome-gnome-shell
```

This is an additional program that enables direct downloading from the website.

20.1.2. Extensions in Synaptic

You select the extension on the website, remember the name and then search for it in **Synaptic**.

In this way, you save the steps that are necessary to install extensions via an add-on directly from the browser.
However, the choice is limited this way.

Search in Synaptic for
gnome-shell-extensions.

Keep in mind that none of the extensions available are an official part of Ubuntu.
Therefore, Ubuntu does not guarantee smooth functioning.
Therefore, use this additional software only if you need it.

20.1.3. The Arc Menu

If you prefer a traditional application menu, then the **ArcMenu** extension may be suitable for you.

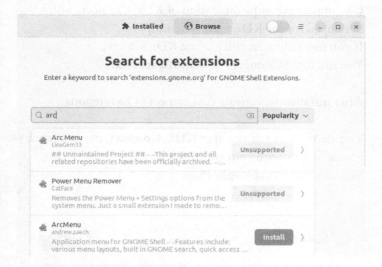

Activities is replaced by a traditional application menu.
ArcMenu is very intuitive and self-explanatory.
Activities Overview takes you back to the activities view.

The cogwheel symbol takes you to extensive settings for the Arc menu.

21. Synchronisation with the Smartphone

GSConnect is an extension that connects Android Devices with your operating system.

GSConnect is a implementation of KDE Connect, which was developed for the KDE Plasma desktop.

If you use Kubuntu, you can use KDE Connect.

You install GSConnect via **Ubuntu software**.

After installation, activate GSConnect in **Extensions**.

You need to install the app **KDE Connect** on your smartphone to sync with your computer.

You can find it on **Google Play.**

22. Useful additional Programs

22.1. Office

22.1.1. Focuswriter

Focuswriter is designed to enable distraction-free writing. It is primarily designed for authors who write longer texts. The user interface is very basic.

You can show the menu bar permanently if you like, but this is not default.
A particularly motivating feature for authors is that they can set themselves daily goals. If these are achieved, the success is stored in a database.
A daily goal can be a certain number of words written (1000 in the example) or a set amount of time you want to spend on writing.

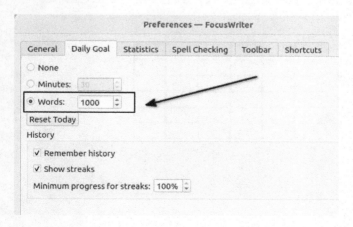

22.1.2. Scribus

Scribus is a layout and typesetting program for desktop publishing.
It is comparable to **InDesign**.

With this program you can construct very elaborate single pages with text and graphics and then combine them into multipage documents.

Many things are very difficult to implement in the same way in word processing programs.

However, you need to familiarise yourself with the structure and handling of Scribus.

Scribus is available in Ubuntu 22.04 in version 1.5.8.

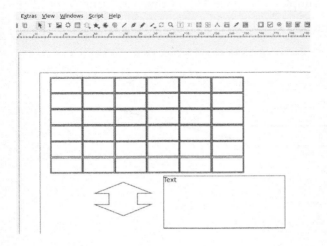

22.1.3. Calibre

With **Calibre** it is possible to archive **eBooks** in all available formats and read them on screen.

Common formats are, for example, **epub** (Tolino etc.) and **mobi** (Kindle).

Metadata (author names, titles, year of publication, etc.) can be adjusted as desired.

In addition, books can also be converted.

So you can convert a book in epub format to mobi format and vice versa.

PDF and even text files can also be converted into eBook formats.

Calibre is thus a good tool for digital book content.

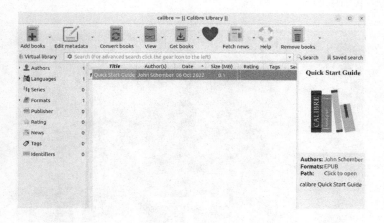

22.1.4. Text Editor Nano

Nano does not require a graphical environment and is therefore suitable for working directly in the shell.

Nano can be opened in the terminal.

Nano is very lightweight and therefore consumes hardly any resources.

Open **Nano** in the terminal with the command `nano`, followed by the path of the file you want to open.

Nano is controlled exclusively via the keyboard.

You move through a document with the arrow keys.

You save a document with

[Ctrl] + [O] and confirm with ENTER.

You leave the editor with

[Ctrl] + [X]

Alternatives: vim, emacs, leafpad, pluma, geany

22.2. Graphics

22.2.1. GIMP

GIMP is a program similar to Adobe Photoshop.

The somewhat strange name comes from the fact that it is actually the abbreviation of
GNU **I**MAGE **M**ANIPULATION **P**ROGRAM

With GIMP, images can be optimised in many ways through the use of countless filters.
It is also possible to create layers.
Additional high-quality filters are optionally available as plugins.
Ubuntu 22.04 offers GIMP 2.10 in the package sources.

GIMP is also available for Windows and OSX.

22.2.2. Darktable

Darktable is comparable to **Lightroom**.
This program specialises in editing image files.

Unlike GIMP, there is no option to create layers.
It is also not possible to insert text.
On the other hand, **Darktable** scores with sophisticated functions such as exposure correction.

It is very intuitive.

In the middle you can see the currently loaded image, on the right side the filters available.

Darktable is also available for Windows and OSX.

22.2.3. Krita

Krita is a sophisticated drawing and painting program.

With the appropriate knowledge of the programme and an artistic streak, very attractive computer drawings can be created.

Krita is also available for Windows and OSX.

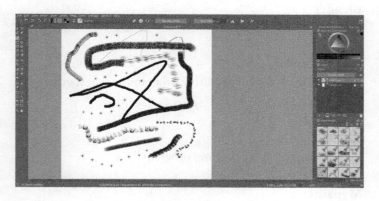

German language packages must be installed for **Krita.**

To do this, execute the following command in the terminal:

```
sudo apt install krita-l10n
```

22.2.4. Other Graphics Programs

Shotwell
Shotwell is a photo organisation program

Inkscape
Inkscape is a vector-based drawing program

Blender
Blender creates 3D objects

Rawtherapee
Rawtherapee is an image editing programme that specialises in RAW files.

Pinta
Pinta is a simple image editing program

Mypaint
Mypaint is a simple drawing program

Tuxpaint
Tuxpaint is a drawing program for children.

Simple-Scan
Simple-Scan connects the scanner to the Linux operating system.

Flameshot
Flameshot is a programme that allows you to take screenshots.

22.3. Video Editing

22.3.1. KDENLIVE

KDENLIVE is considered the most sophisticated video editing program available free of charge for Linux distributions.

It can be used to realise elaborate video cuts.
In addition to the numerous editing functions, a variety of effects are available.
These include the integration of text, numerous transitions and alienation effects.

The interface consists of a preview window and a timeline with tracks.

After a certain period of familiarisation, working with KDENLIVE goes smoothly.

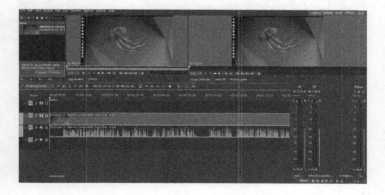

22.3.2. OpenShot

OpenShot is not as lavishly equipped as KDENLIVE.

OpenShot comes with simple editing functions and a smaller number of effects.

If you use OpenShot you don't have to learn as much as if you use KDENLIVE.

OpenShot is very intuitive to use and is sufficient for small projects that get by with few effects.

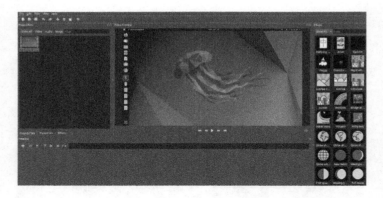

22.3.3. Other video editing programmes

- Shotcut
- Avidemux
- DaVinciResolve
- Lightworks (proprietary)

22.4. Audio

22.4.1. Audacity

With **Audacity,** audio recordings can be edited and changed in many ways.
The audio file is displayed as a waveform on a timeline.
In this way, it is possible to cut with pinpoint accuracy and remove interfering parts.

But the file itself can also be manipulated.
Equalizer and compressor are part of the basic tools.
In addition, it is possible, among other things, to eliminate background noise.

Audacity is excellent for recording and editing audio files.

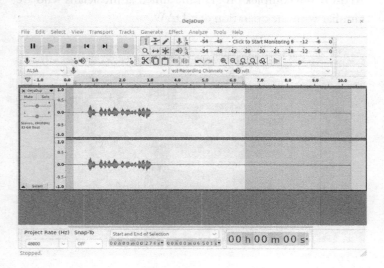

22.4.2. Ardour

Ardour goes one step further than Audacity.

This allows multi-track recordings to be made just like in a recording studio.

Comparable commercial programmes are Cubase by Steinberg or Logic by Apple.

Even if the range of functions does not quite reach the products mentioned, Ardour is an astonishingly mature program that is well equipped for semi-professional tasks.

In addition to the basic functions of recording, playback and mixing, Ardour's range of functions can be considerably extended by plug-ins.

Ardour is a complex programme aimed at musicians who are familiar with the operation of a DAW.

22.4.3. MuseScore

MuseScore is aimed at musicians who need a music notation program.

The notes are inserted at the desired position in the given staff by mouse click or midi input.
Complex scores for several instruments can also be created.
Adding text is also possible without any problems.

A wide range of formatting options leave plenty of scope for individual design options.

A listening function rounds off the thoroughly positive picture.

22.5. Internet

Browser

Many common browsers are available for Linux, which are also widely used under Windows.

The best known is probably **Firefox**. This is already pre-installed in Ubuntu 22.04.

There is also **Chromium** (an open source compliant version of Google Chrome), **Opera**, **Vivaldi** and many more.

However, Chromium can only be installed as a snap under Ubuntu!

If you value anonymity, the **Tor** Browser is the best choice.
Not available is **Safari,** the default browser of MacOS.
The introduction of **Edge** for Linux is at least being considered.
Google is most often used as a search engine, but there are also alternatives that are a little more privacy-conscious.
These include **DuckDuckGo** and **Startpage**.

You can easily set these alternatives as the default search engine in your browser.

Evolution is available as an alternative for the email-client Thunderbird. It also offers a planner, address book and notebook.

22.6. Audio and Video Player

A wide selection of audio and video players is available in Linux.

However, it is often unavoidable that additional codecs must be installed so that all formats can be recognized and played.

This is not a problem with Ubuntu if you have selected the inclusion of **third-party software** during installation.

If you have not checked this box, you may have to install codecs later.

Ubuntu offers very good players for audio and video with **Rhythmbox** and **Videos.**

A good alternative, but one that must be installed later, is the program VLC.

This application can play both videos and audio files.

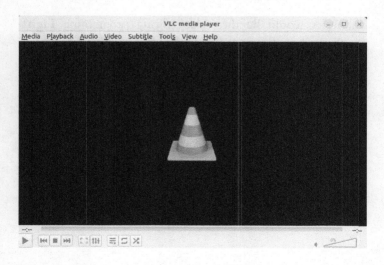

22.7. Third-party Software

The official package sources of Ubuntu 22.04 generally contain mainly free software.
If the software is from a third party, it is marked accordingly.

Third-party software is proprietary (i.e. with closed source code), but can still often be used under Ubuntu 22.04.

If these are drivers for specific hardware or codecs for playing audio and video files, they are usually free of charge.
In addition, there are applications that run in Linux but are still chargeable.
Mostly, however, there are slimmed-down free versions of these programs.

Examples would be the video editing programme **Lightworks** or the office suite **Softmaker Pro**.

You get these programs directly from the developers and receive an activation code after registering and paying.

This type of program has not yet been able to establish itself. The selection of free applications, most of which disclose the source code, is usually quite good enough in quality for the casual user.

23. Windows Programs in Linux

There is no direct way to install **Windows applications** on a Linux operating system.

Programs such as Microsoft Office or Adobe Photoshop are not provided for Linux.

However, there are ways in which you can still use these applications inLinux.

However, smooth functioning is not guaranteed in all cases.

Basically, there are two fundamentally different ways you can try.

23.1. Wine and PlayOnLinux

Wine creates a Windows runtime environment on your Linux computer.

This attempts to recreate a Windows environment as realistically as possible.

This works well for some applications, less so for others.

Install the Wine frontend **PlayOnLinux.**

You can also install **Wine** itself, but PlayOnLinux makes it easier to use the Wine environment with intuitive graphically appealing menu navigation.

After the first start, an appealing user menu awaits you, which gives a first overview of the possibilities of PlayOnLinux.

The applications recommended by POL are divided into categories.

In **Office** you will find several versions of Microsoft Office, Photoshop CS 6, Lightroom 5, Ableton Live 9 and Reaper 4.

In addition, many Windows games are also included.

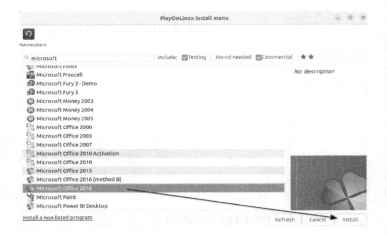

Please bear in mind that you will always need an original DVD/CD and also the activation key to install an application. Once you have decided on a program, start the installation with the **Install** button, which you will find at the bottom right.

During installation, you may be informed that additional files are required for the process to be completed successfully.
In this case, follow the instructions that are displayed to you.

It is advisable to visit to Wine's website.

https://www.winehq.org/

AppDB: Here you can find out whether the application you want to install is currently well supported by Wine.

For this purpose, there is a ranking based on the experiences of users.

Platinum is the best rating, but there are also applications that are rated **Garbage**.

You will also find tips and information on what you need to consider for a successful installation of a program.

PlayOnLinux lists many well-known and frequently used Windows programs in the categories.
However, you can also try to install an application that is not listed here.
To do this, click on the bottom left
Install a programme that is **not listed.**
This can work in some cases, but it usually involves some research work to find the best way.
However, there are also applications that cannot be installed in this way or that can only be used to a limited extent despite successful installation.

If you are not successful with **Wine**, you can try the commercial programme **Crossover.**
However, this is not available free of charge and there is no guarantee that it will work.

23.2. Virtual Machine (Virtual Box)

Another way to get Windows programs or even MacOS applications running is to set up a virtual machine.

On this way not only a runtime environment is set up, as is the case with Wine.

Here you install a real Windows or MacOS within your Linux operating system, which is completely independent.

In this case you also need an original CD/DVD and the activation key.

You must provide this operating system, which runs in parallel with Ubuntu, with sufficient computing power and RAM, otherwise it can also only be used to a very limited extent.

For a Windows virtual machine, you should allocate at least 50 GB of your hard disk space.

Therefore, increase the value suggested during installation accordingly.

There are various solutions for creating a virtual machine on your system.

One of the most widely used is **Virtual Box**.

You will find this program in the repositories of Ubuntu and can thus conveniently install it via Ubuntu software.

On some computers, virtual machine support must be activated in the BIOS!

After starting Virtual Box, click on the NEW button.

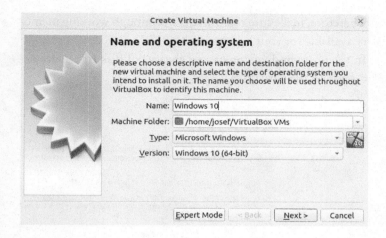

Give the operating system an individual name and confirm with **Next**!

Increase the Memory size within the green range.

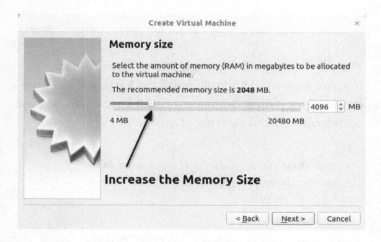

The value selected here is no longer available to your main system as soon as you start the virtual machine.

Therefore, make sure that there is still enough working memory available for your host system!

In the next window you can set the size of disk (the space occupied on the hard disk).

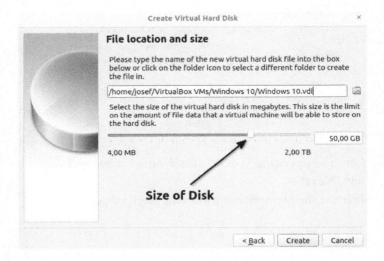

You will then be guided through the installation process.

It makes sense to additionally install the **Virtual Box Extensions** and the **(Guest Additions) Guest Extensions,** as these considerably expand the range of functions.

> *Virtual Box is also available for Windows and MacOS.*
> *So you can also go the other way and install Ubuntu in the Virtual Box under Windows.*

An alternative to Virtual Box is **GNOME Boxes.**
This is easier to use, but its functions are also limited.
You can find **Gnome boxes** in **Ubuntu software**.

24. The Terminal

The terminal is the interface that connects the user with all the functional possibilities provided by the operating system.

For each action you want to perform, there is a specific command.
This command is executed by entering it in the command line and then confirming it with ENTER.
To open the terminal, go to the application overview and type in the first letters.
Terminal is now listed as an application.
After starting the terminal, you will only see a single line.
It shows your user name in the first place, followed by the name you have given your computer.

The username in the example is *max*.
The user *max* is logged on to (@)*max-ubuntu*.

The following character ~ is called a **tilde.**
It stands for the location within the computer where we are at the moment.

~ is the abbreviation for the home folder.

At the position where the cursor is, you can now enter the required command.

Some important examples:

Updating the repositories
```
sudo apt update
```

Updating the system
```
sudo apt upgrade
```

Installing a program
```
sudo apt install [program name]
```

You will be asked for the password after entering these commands.

This is necessary for security reasons, so that no unauthorised access can be made to your system in this way.

The list of available commands is endless.

You can copy, move and also delete files. You can also use the terminal as a file manager, as you can query the contents of directories with simple commands.

In many cases, the terminal is even the more effective and faster way to execute tasks.

However it is very important that you know the commands and that you are able to use the keyboard quickly.

25. Ubuntu Flavours

There are also other official versions of Ubuntu.
These use a different desktop instead of GNOME.

You can choose between

KUBUNTU
> *Ubuntu with KDE Plasma*

UBUNTU MATE
> *Ubuntu with Mate Desktop*

UBUNTU BUDGIE
> *Ubuntu with Budgie Desktop*

XUBUNTU
> *Ubuntu with XFCE desktop*

LUBUNTU
> *Ubuntu with LXQt desktop*

UBUNTU STUDIO
> *Ubuntu for multimedia applications*

In addition, there are numerous independent distributions based on Ubuntu.

ELEMENTARY OS, LINUX MINT, KDE NEON

26. Outlook

Currently the following versions are supported:

- Ubuntu 18.04 LTS until April 2023
- Ubuntu 20.04 LTS until April 2025
- Ubuntu 22.04 LTS until April 2027
- Ubuntu 22.10 until July 2023

It will be followed in April 2023 by Ubuntu 23.04 with short-term support (9 months).

The next LTS version is Ubuntu 24.04. This will again be supported for 5 years (until 2029) and will be released in April 2024.

With the release of Ubuntu 24.04 you can decide whether you want to use Ubuntu 22.04 until the end of support in 2027 or switch to the newer LTS version 24.04.

It is also possible to switch to the short-term versions and then upgrade to the next after expiry.

However, in this case you leave the LTS path.

Also available from this author:

Ubuntu 18.04 : Quick guide for beginners
Arch Linux : Quick guide for beginners

Soon to come:

The Linux Terminal - Quick Guide fo beginners

Also:

Serenity through stoicism
The wisdom of Epictetus, Seneca and Marcus Aurelius

Conversation with Seneca

Made in the USA
Las Vegas, NV
10 December 2023